There Is No Such Thing as Job Security; There Is Skill Security

There Is No Such Thing as Job Security; There Is Skill Security

Contents

Copyright © 2024 by Di Tran Enterprise 3

Introduction: No Such Thing as Job Security, Only Skill Security 5

Chapter 1: People Last Forever, Jobs Do Not 13

Chapter 2: Apply for Jobs, Practice Interviews 22

Chapter 3: Learn Continuously, Add Value 33

Chapter 4: Work for Yourself, Not Just the Company 50

Chapter 5: AI and The Transparency of Productivity 64

Chapter 6: Adaptability Is Your Greatest Asset 80

Chapter 7: Networking: Your Lifelong Security Net 98

Chapter 8: Side Projects and Freelancing for Security 107

Chapter 9: Upskill for the Future: Continuous Learning Plans 124

Chapter 10: Own Your Career Growth: Measure, Track, and Improve 142

Embracing Self: The True Identity Beyond Jobs – A Dedication to Brian Keinsley and Thomas Noland 152

POEM: God, Life is Short 154

The End 155

**There Is No Such Thing as Job Security;
There Is Skill Security**

Copyright © 2024 by Di Tran Enterprise

All rights reserved. No part of this publication may be reproduced, distributed, or transmitted in any form or by any means, including photocopying, recording, or other electronic or mechanical methods, without the prior written permission of the publisher, except in the case of brief quotations embodied in critical reviews and certain other noncommercial uses permitted by copyright law.

The information contained in this book is intended for educational and inspirational purposes only. It is sold with the understanding that the publisher and author are not engaged in rendering psychological, counseling, or other professional services. If expert assistance is required, the services of a competent professional should be sought.

This publication is designed to provide accurate and authoritative information in regard to the subject matter covered. It is presented with the understanding that the author and publisher are not engaged in rendering personal, professional, or any other kind of advice. The reader should consult his or her medical, legal, financial, or other competent professional before adopting any of the suggestions in this book or drawing inferences from it.

There Is No Such Thing as Job Security; There Is Skill Security

This publication reflects the author's views, experiences, and opinions. It is intended to provide helpful and informative material on the subjects addressed in the publication. The author and publisher shall have neither liability nor responsibility to any person or entity with respect to any loss, damage, or injury caused, or alleged to be caused, directly or indirectly by the information contained in this book.

While the author has made every effort to ensure the accuracy and completeness of the information contained in this publication, we assume no responsibility for errors, inaccuracies, omissions, or any inconsistency herein. Any slights of people or organizations are unintentional.

There Is No Such Thing as Job Security; There Is Skill Security

Introduction: No Such Thing as Job Security, Only Skill Security

When I first arrived in America in 1995, I didn't speak a word of English. As a Vietnamese immigrant, I found myself in ESL (English as a Second Language) classes, struggling while most of my classmates mastered the language in just a year or two. For me, it took more than six long years to finally feel comfortable with English—and even then, I was slow compared to others.

But that wasn't the only challenge. In college, I was no star student. I pursued a degree in computer engineering at the University of Louisville's Speed School of Engineering, but my grades were mediocre at best: C's, C-'s, and the occasional C+. Many of my classmates were excelling, but for me, the struggle was real, constant, and humbling.

It took me six months after graduation to land my first job, despite having built numerous software projects during my internships, including at UPS. I began my professional journey with Humana in 2006, and my first corporate mentor, Bobbie Binggeli, who reported to Peter Leach, believed in me enough to send me to offsite training with top vendors. From there, I rewrote multiple software systems for Humana's Network Operations Center (NOC), and my career started to take off rapidly. I was promoted yearly, but I never took that as a sign of security.

There Is No Such Thing as Job Security; There Is Skill Security

The Myth of Job Security: A Personal Journey

Despite my promotions, I never believed in the concept of job security. Even as I was promoted, I kept going to school and applying for new jobs, attending interviews almost monthly. I wanted to stay sharp, keep my skills fresh, and understand what the market wanted. This constant practice helped me not only as an interviewee but also as an interviewer. I always had a foot in both worlds: learning, growing, and staying connected to the job market.

Over time, I realized that this mindset gave me an edge. I learned early on that job security was an illusion, and that the only security anyone could have was in their skills. I moved to new roles within Humana every two years, and if the company didn't have the position I wanted, I moved on to another company. I never became complacent. Moving to new positions allowed me to learn new things, meet new people, and grow my expertise.

Through this journey, I gained something invaluable: adaptability. I learned how to complete complex software projects, master new programming languages, and write software architecture documentation. I learned to lead teams, present ideas, and draw system diagrams. I learned that real security comes from continuously evolving.

The Importance of Leadership and Mentorship

There Is No Such Thing as Job Security; There Is Skill Security

As I climbed the corporate ladder, I began to realize that technical skills alone weren't enough. I needed to learn about leadership. So I took a bold step: I reached out to Humana's Senior Vice Presidents, asking them to mentor me.

Thomas Noland was one of those senior executives, and he mentored me in corporate communication—how to speak and present myself at an executive level. Brian Keinsley, who was three levels above me, also became my mentor. Both of these men opened doors for me that I never would have found on my own. They didn't just teach me about leadership and communication; they taught me about navigating corporate life with resilience and humility.

Working on projects was no longer just about promotions for me. It was about boosting my resume and real skills. Promotion came naturally, not because I sought it, but because my skills and contributions were undeniable. I took on bigger and bigger projects, learning how to manage complexity and lead teams to success.

When I reached the top of my engineering career at Humana, I was given the title of Principal Software Architect, the highest engineering role available. Out of 7,000+ engineers at the company, I was one of the top three. But even at the pinnacle of my technical career, I knew I couldn't rest.

There Is No Such Thing as Job Security; There Is Skill Security

The Wake-Up Call: Humana's Corporate Changes

In 2019, Humana underwent a wave of corporate changes, and despite my high-ranking position, I found myself laid off during the company's yearly evaluation. I was labeled a "low performer," which was far from the truth. It was a painful realization—job security truly doesn't exist, even at the top. No matter your title, your value, or your contributions, corporations move according to their own needs and priorities.

I reached out to Brian Keinsley for advice. He counseled me not to resign but to let things play out in the company's terms. Despite his mentorship, I was still laid off for the first time in my career. It was a humbling moment. I had always moved jobs by choice, but this time, the decision was out of my hands. I was no longer employed as a top engineer, and I had to accept that my identity couldn't be tied to a title or a corporate structure.

I learned an important lesson: job titles, prestige, and status are fleeting. What truly matters is the impact we have on others, and the skills we build along the way. My mentors, Brian and Thomas, had taught me that leadership isn't just about holding a position—it's about adapting, learning, and continuously improving.

Before AI: Millions of Lines of Code Written By Hand

There Is No Such Thing as Job Security; There Is Skill Security

Before the era of AI, I wrote millions of lines of code myself, delivering countless systems and projects. Every line of code was written manually, every test case carefully crafted, every piece of test data manually created, and every deployment done step-by-step. In today's world, all those processes are automated. AI generates code, writes test cases, creates test data, runs the tests, and even deploys the software from start to finish.

The IT industry is at the most pivotal point in history. We are now building systems that automate what once took months or years to develop by hand. AI is not only replacing workers but also revealing inefficiencies in real time, exposing areas of waste and unproductive habits across industries. This is particularly evident in sectors like IT, writing, legal, and even healthcare and education. Teachers, professors, and doctors are also facing the pressure of AI-driven innovation.

Adapting is no longer a choice—it's a necessity. Most of us weren't raised in an environment that prepared us for this level of technological disruption. In the USA, job security was foundational, and government and corporate policies have long leaned in that direction. But now, everything has changed, and it's urgent that we adapt faster than ever before, even though it's not easy.

The Path Forward: Skill Security, Not Job Security

There Is No Such Thing as Job Security; There Is Skill Security

After being laid off, I could have crumbled. But I had been preparing for this moment for years. While my corporate job was gone, I had built other streams of income. I had been working seven days a week, running beauty businesses and working as a nail technician on the weekends. I wasn't reliant on a single company for my livelihood, and that financial security gave me the freedom to pivot quickly.

I also had the skills to back me up. I had spent years learning new programming languages, developing software, and honing my leadership abilities. The job may have been gone, but my skills remained. This is the essence of what I call "skill security." It's the idea that while job security is an illusion, the security we create through our skills, adaptability, and constant learning is very real.

As I wrote this book, I reflected on the importance of resilience. Life doesn't come with guarantees, and careers certainly don't. But if we commit ourselves to continuous learning, to adding value wherever we go, and to building a diverse set of skills, we can weather any storm. My mentors, Brian and Thomas, believed in me when I was just starting out, and I carry their lessons with me every day.

Their passing, and my own journey, have shown me that the only true security we have in life is what we invest in ourselves. We live in a world where technology, markets, and industries are constantly evolving, and we have to

There Is No Such Thing as Job Security; There Is Skill Security

evolve with them. The only way to secure your future is to ensure that your skills are always in demand, and that you are always ready for whatever comes next.

Conclusion

This book is not just a collection of strategies for navigating your career—it's a testament to the power of resilience, adaptability, and continuous learning. My story, like many others, is one of struggle, failure, and perseverance. From arriving in America with no English skills to becoming a top engineer at Humana, my journey has taught me that nothing is permanent, especially jobs.

But there is something permanent: **skill security**. By developing your abilities, staying adaptable, and continuously learning, you can ensure that you'll always have a place in the workforce. It's not about relying on a company to secure your future; it's about relying on yourself.

As you read this book, I hope you'll be inspired to take control of your own career. Don't chase job security—it doesn't exist. Chase skill security, because that's something no one can take away from you.

*There Is No Such Thing as Job Security;
There Is Skill Security*

Chapter 1: People Last Forever, Jobs Do Not

In today's fast-evolving job market, it's becoming clearer that job security, once considered a cornerstone of professional success, is no longer guaranteed. What lasts is not the job title or the company logo on your paycheck—it's your personal brand, your character, your ability to adapt, and your capacity for human connection. People last forever, but jobs do not. This chapter dives deep into the importance of cultivating soft skills like communication, writing, presenting, and emotional intelligence, which form the bedrock of professional success and personal fulfillment. As the world around us shifts, these skills remain the constant foundation that helps you grow both professionally and personally.

Soft Skills: The Timeless Foundation

While hard skills like coding, data analysis, or technical proficiency are important, they often have a shelf life. With advancements in technology and shifts in industry, hard skills must be constantly updated. Soft skills, on the other hand, are timeless. They form the core of how you interact with people, how you lead, how you communicate your value, and how you build relationships.

There Is No Such Thing as Job Security; There Is Skill Security

A study by LinkedIn's 2019 Global Talent Trends report revealed that 92% of talent professionals and hiring managers consider soft skills equally or more important than hard skills. The same study found that the most sought-after soft skills are creativity, persuasion, collaboration, adaptability, and emotional intelligence.

Soft skills such as empathy, communication, and the ability to work in a team have been linked not only to career success but also to greater job satisfaction and personal well-being. People who possess strong soft skills are better equipped to navigate the complexities of human relationships, resolve conflicts, and inspire others. In contrast, employees with strong technical skills but poor soft skills may struggle to adapt to changing work environments or build strong professional relationships.

Communication: The Cornerstone of Influence

Effective communication, whether written, spoken, or non-verbal, remains one of the most crucial soft skills. It's how you articulate your ideas, influence others, and share your vision. Your ability to communicate well can set you apart in any industry, regardless of your technical or academic background.

For instance, even though I struggled academically and took longer to master English than my peers, my ability to improve my communication skills over time became a key

There Is No Such Thing as Job Security; There Is Skill Security

driver of my success. I reached out to senior leaders, sent emails to top executives, and requested mentorship—all because I had built the confidence to communicate effectively, despite the language barrier.

The ability to communicate well also gives you the flexibility to navigate changes in your job. Whether you're interviewing for a new position, presenting to an executive team, or simply explaining a problem to a colleague, how you communicate defines how others perceive you. And as we know, perception often leads to opportunities.

Writing: Your Personal Brand in Print

Writing is another vital aspect of communication that has an immense impact on your career. With so much of today's work being remote or digital, writing is often the primary way you represent yourself. Emails, reports, proposals, and presentations are all extensions of your personal brand.

Strong writing skills can make the difference between being understood clearly and leaving people confused or frustrated. Clear writing reflects clear thinking, and when you're able to convey complex ideas simply and effectively, you position yourself as someone who brings clarity and value to your organization.

In a digital-first world, where many interactions are through screens rather than face-to-face, your written word

There Is No Such Thing as Job Security; There Is Skill Security

may be the only way people experience your thought process. Whether you're applying for jobs, proposing a project, or communicating across teams, your writing speaks volumes about your professionalism, attention to detail, and intellectual rigor.

Presenting: Delivering Ideas That Stick

Presenting goes beyond formal presentations at conferences or meetings. It's about how you deliver information, how you carry yourself, and how well you articulate your thoughts to influence others. Effective presenters are more than just speakers—they're storytellers who engage their audience, convey information with passion, and leave a lasting impact.

Good presentation skills help you convey your expertise in a way that resonates with others. Whether you're pitching a new idea to your team, leading a client meeting, or introducing yourself in an interview, the ability to present well can elevate your career to new heights.

For example, I discovered the power of presentation early in my career. When I started presenting my software solutions to senior leaders at Humana, I wasn't just showing technical details—I was telling a story about how these systems would change operations and save time. It wasn't just about what I built, but about why it mattered and how it could improve the organization. My ability to

There Is No Such Thing as Job Security; There Is Skill Security

present ideas compellingly allowed me to gain trust, secure larger projects, and climb the corporate ladder.

Emotional Intelligence: The Key to Meaningful Relationships

Emotional intelligence (EQ) refers to your ability to understand and manage your own emotions and the emotions of others. It's the glue that holds relationships together in the workplace and beyond. High EQ individuals are skilled at navigating difficult conversations, managing conflicts, showing empathy, and motivating others.

Daniel Goleman, who popularized the concept of emotional intelligence, found that EQ can be a better predictor of success than IQ in many leadership roles. Leaders with high emotional intelligence are more effective at influencing, persuading, and managing teams. They understand how to engage others, inspire trust, and create environments where people feel valued.

In my own career, I saw firsthand how emotional intelligence played a critical role. My technical skills could only take me so far. It was my ability to empathize with colleagues, understand what executives needed, and motivate teams that allowed me to grow as a leader. When I began managing projects, I realized that the success of those projects didn't depend solely on the quality of the code, but on how well I could manage the people building

There Is No Such Thing as Job Security; There Is Skill Security

it. By cultivating emotional intelligence, I built stronger teams, resolved conflicts, and gained the respect of my peers and leaders alike.

Cultivating Care and Love in All Interactions

One of the most overlooked soft skills is the ability to genuinely care about others. It's easy to become consumed by the technical aspects of work—deadlines, goals, and results. But the most successful professionals are those who bring humanity into the workplace. They take the time to listen to others, build meaningful relationships, and demonstrate care and love in their interactions.

The Harvard Business Review published a study showing that employees who feel cared for and valued by their employers are more engaged, productive, and loyal. Companies that cultivate a culture of care are not only more successful but also more resilient in times of crisis.

Showing care in the workplace isn't just about being nice. It's about understanding that every interaction has the potential to either lift someone up or bring them down. When you prioritize care, you create a positive ripple effect that improves not just the morale of your team, but the quality of the work you produce together.

Self-Boost: Building Self-Esteem and Value

There Is No Such Thing as Job Security; There Is Skill Security

One of the core themes of this chapter is the idea of boosting your own self-value. Jobs may come and go, but your self-esteem and self-worth are your true assets. Developing soft skills not only helps you excel in the workplace, but also builds your confidence. When you know that you can communicate effectively, present with impact, and manage your emotions, you become more secure in yourself.

Building self-value requires constant learning, practicing new skills, and pushing yourself out of your comfort zone. The process may be slow and incremental, but with each new skill mastered, your sense of self-worth grows. This self-boost is essential, especially in times of uncertainty, when job security seems elusive.

The Power of Self-Identity

Your job does not define you—your skills, character, and values do. As you navigate the ups and downs of your career, it's essential to build a strong sense of self-identity. This means understanding who you are beyond your job title. What are your strengths? What are your values? How do you want to impact the world?

Your soft skills, such as empathy, communication, and leadership, help shape this self-identity. They allow you to express yourself authentically and connect with others on a deeper level. By investing in soft skills, you're investing in

There Is No Such Thing as Job Security; There Is Skill Security

your own personal growth, which in turn leads to professional success.

Studies and Statistics to Support Soft Skills Development

Numerous studies have shown the importance of soft skills in career development:

- **McKinsey & Company's Future of Work Report** highlighted that by 2030, demand for soft skills will grow across industries, with a 22% increase in jobs requiring social and emotional skills.

- A **LinkedIn Learning Survey** revealed that 57% of senior leaders believe soft skills are more important than hard skills.

- According to the **World Economic Forum's Future of Jobs Report**, emotional intelligence, creativity, and leadership are among the top 10 skills that will be critical for success in the coming decade.

These findings reinforce the notion that while jobs may not last forever, the skills you build today—particularly your soft skills—will sustain your career for the long haul.

Conclusion: People Last Forever, Jobs Do Not

There Is No Such Thing as Job Security; There Is Skill Security

As the world of work continues to evolve, job security will remain a fleeting concept. But the skills you develop, the relationships you build, and the impact you make on others will last forever. Soft skills like communication, emotional intelligence, and leadership aren't just tools for career advancement—they're the foundation of a life well-lived.

Investing in these skills ensures that no matter where your career takes you, you will always bring value to the table. Your job may not last forever, but the person you become and the skills you develop along the way will stay with you, opening doors and creating opportunities that go far beyond any single role.

There Is No Such Thing as Job Security; There Is Skill Security

Chapter 2: Apply for Jobs, Practice Interviews

In today's fast-paced and ever-evolving job market, one of the most effective strategies to stay ahead is to continuously apply for jobs and practice interviewing. This practice isn't just for those actively seeking new employment but for anyone who wants to stay competitive, hone their skills, and stay current with market demands. Applying for jobs and interviewing regularly is more than just about landing a new position—it's about boosting self-esteem, improving self-value, enhancing your skills, and fostering your identity as someone who is always in demand.

In this chapter, we will explore why the process of applying for jobs and attending interviews should be a regular part of your professional development, regardless of your employment status. We'll also discuss the power of human interaction during interviews and how this experience can significantly enhance your interpersonal skills, self-confidence, and adaptability.

Why You Should Always Apply for Jobs

In a world where technology, markets, and industries change rapidly, it's crucial to never become too comfortable in a single role or position. While it may seem

There Is No Such Thing as Job Security; There Is Skill Security

counterintuitive to apply for jobs when you're not looking for one, the benefits of this practice go far beyond job offers. Here's why:

1. **Stay Updated on Market Trends**: Every time you apply for a job, you gain insights into what companies are looking for, what skills are in demand, and where the industry is heading. By regularly reviewing job postings, you can keep a finger on the pulse of the market. This allows you to continuously assess whether your skill set is still relevant and what areas you might need to improve upon.

2. **Benchmark Your Skills**: By engaging with the job market, you can assess how your skills stack up against industry standards. This ongoing evaluation ensures you never fall behind, giving you the opportunity to upskill when necessary and stay competitive.

3. **Boost Self-Esteem and Self-Worth**: Just the act of applying for jobs and going through the interview process can be empowering. Even if you don't get the job, the experience helps you practice communicating your value, thereby boosting your confidence and self-esteem. Every rejection is not a failure but a stepping stone to improving how you present yourself.

There Is No Such Thing as Job Security; There Is Skill Security

4. **Negotiate Better in Your Current Role**: By understanding what's out there and knowing your market value, you can negotiate better terms—whether that's asking for a raise, discussing a promotion, or requesting additional responsibilities in your current role.

5. **Opportunities for Growth**: Applying for jobs can introduce you to new possibilities that you may not have considered. Even if you're happy where you are, discovering roles with new responsibilities or in different industries can open your mind to other career paths. It's essential to remain open to change, especially in a world where jobs are constantly evolving.

Practicing Interviews: A Skill to Master

Interviewing is one of the most critical human interaction skills you can develop. Whether you're an introvert, extrovert, or somewhere in between, interviews push you to communicate clearly, listen carefully, and interact effectively under pressure. Practicing interviews continuously helps you sharpen these skills.

According to a study published by the *Harvard Business Review*, professionals who regularly participate in interviews—either as interviewers or interviewees—report higher levels of confidence, better communication skills,

There Is No Such Thing as Job Security; There Is Skill Security

and a greater ability to think on their feet. These qualities not only make for successful interviews but also improve overall job performance.

Here are a few reasons why you should continually practice your interview skills:

1. **Sharpen Your Storytelling Abilities**: Interviews require you to explain who you are, what you've accomplished, and why you're a good fit for the role. Regular interviews give you the opportunity to refine this narrative, making it more compelling each time. You learn to connect your past experiences to future goals more effectively.

2. **Improving Emotional Intelligence**: An interview is not just about showcasing your qualifications—it's about connecting with your interviewer. This requires emotional intelligence (EQ), which refers to your ability to understand and manage your emotions and those of others. Practicing interviews helps you develop your EQ by making you more aware of how your words, tone, and body language affect the person sitting across from you.

3. **Developing a Growth Mindset**: Interviews force you to reflect on your career trajectory, goals, and personal growth. This continuous reflection encourages a growth mindset, where you focus on

There Is No Such Thing as Job Security; There Is Skill Security

learning, adapting, and improving rather than clinging to the security of a fixed position. A study by Carol Dweck, a renowned psychologist at Stanford University, found that individuals with a growth mindset tend to achieve more in their careers because they view challenges and setbacks as opportunities for growth rather than threats to their self-worth.

4. **Reduce Interview Anxiety**: Many people experience anxiety during interviews, especially if they haven't interviewed in a while. By regularly attending interviews, you reduce that anxiety. Repetition makes the process feel more familiar, helping you feel more relaxed and confident.

5. **Hone Active Listening**: Active listening is an essential skill during interviews. It's not enough to simply wait for your turn to speak—you must listen carefully to what the interviewer is asking, respond thoughtfully, and ask follow-up questions. Practicing interviews helps you become a more attentive listener, a skill that is valuable not just in interviews but in all areas of life.

The Role of Self-Value and Self-Esteem in Interviews

One of the most important benefits of continuously applying for jobs and practicing interviews is the effect it

There Is No Such Thing as Job Security; There Is Skill Security

has on your self-value and self-esteem. When you regularly engage with the job market, you're reminded of your value. You learn how to articulate your skills and experiences in a way that demonstrates your worth. This act of self-promotion is crucial for boosting self-esteem.

In fact, a study by the *University of California, Berkeley* found that individuals who practice self-promotion in interviews are more likely to experience higher levels of job satisfaction and career success. This is because they have learned how to communicate their value and take ownership of their accomplishments. Practicing interviews reinforces your self-worth, helping you internalize the idea that you are a valuable asset to any team or organization.

Moreover, continuously applying for jobs and attending interviews helps you develop a stronger sense of self-identity. When you are forced to explain who you are, what you've done, and where you want to go, you become more in tune with your personal and professional identity. You gain clarity about your strengths, your goals, and what sets you apart from others.

Statistics and Studies Supporting Continuous Interviewing

Several studies have highlighted the benefits of continuous job applications and interviews:

There Is No Such Thing as Job Security; There Is Skill Security

- **LinkedIn's Workforce Learning Report (2021)** emphasized that people who regularly engage in upskilling and job search activities are more adaptable to market changes and economic shifts. These individuals are more likely to be promoted or given new opportunities within their current companies.

- A study by the **Center for Creative Leadership** found that professionals who regularly interview are 70% more likely to be aware of current trends and skill gaps within their industry. This awareness allows them to remain competitive and employable even in fluctuating job markets.

- Research from **Gallup** revealed that individuals who regularly engage in professional development activities, including practicing interviews, report higher levels of career satisfaction and personal fulfillment. This is because they feel more in control of their career trajectory, rather than being at the mercy of their employer's decisions.

Human Interaction: The Value of Practicing Social Skills

Interviews aren't just about landing a job—they're also about developing and practicing your social skills. Human interaction in interviews requires you to be present,

There Is No Such Thing as Job Security; There Is Skill Security

engaged, and aware of the nuances of conversation. Whether you're negotiating a salary or explaining your qualifications, the way you communicate with others is crucial.

The ability to interact effectively with others is often referred to as **social intelligence**. Social intelligence involves understanding social cues, reading body language, and adjusting your communication style to fit the situation. In interviews, you need to adapt quickly to the interviewer's tone, style, and preferences. This adaptability is a key component of social intelligence, and practicing interviews helps you develop it.

Moreover, interviewing regularly helps you build **confidence** in social interactions. Many people feel uncomfortable in situations where they're being evaluated, but regular practice can reduce this discomfort. Over time, you'll find that you're more confident not just in interviews but in all types of social interactions—whether that's networking at an industry event or leading a meeting at work.

The Interviewer's Perspective: Gaining Insights from Both Sides

One of the most valuable aspects of practicing interviews is the opportunity to learn from both sides of the table. By regularly interviewing for new roles, you gain insights into

There Is No Such Thing as Job Security; There Is Skill Security

what interviewers are looking for, how they ask questions, and how they assess candidates. This perspective is invaluable when you find yourself on the other side of the table, conducting interviews or evaluating others in your own organization.

Understanding the interviewer's mindset can give you a significant advantage in future interviews. You'll know what types of answers resonate, how to structure your responses, and what behaviors to avoid. This insight will help you stand out in future interviews and make a lasting impression on potential employers.

Conclusion: Interviews as a Continuous Learning Process

The job market is constantly evolving, and the skills that are in demand today may not be in demand tomorrow. By continuously applying for jobs and practicing interviews, you ensure that you remain competitive, adaptable, and aware of market trends. Regularly engaging with the job market not only improves your chances of landing a new role but also helps you develop essential soft skills like communication, emotional intelligence, and social intelligence.

In addition, the practice of interviewing boosts your self-esteem and self-value, helping you become more confident in your abilities and more aware of your strengths. The

There Is No Such Thing as Job Security; There Is Skill Security

more you interview, the more you understand your worth and the better you become at communicating it to others.

Remember, interviews are not just interviews, they're learning experiences that can elevate your self-confidence, self-worth, and social intelligence. It's a continuous process that refines not only how you present yourself but also how you view your value in the professional world. Regularly applying for jobs and practicing interviews keeps you sharp, aware of market demands, and ready for opportunities that align with your skills and aspirations.

So, don't wait until you need a job—treat interviews as opportunities for growth. They boost your professional value and ensure that your skill set evolves with the times, keeping you adaptable and relevant in the ever-changing world of work.

By embracing the idea that interviews are part of a continuous learning journey, you are preparing yourself for whatever challenges and opportunities may come your way. Whether you are aiming to negotiate for a better position, seeking new experiences, or simply testing the waters, practicing the art of interviews will help you become a better communicator, a more confident individual, and a person who is always ready for the next step.

There Is No Such Thing as Job Security; There Is Skill Security

Chapter 3: Learn Continuously, Add Value

In a world where corporate security is an illusion and market demands are ever-changing, one fact remains constant: **you must keep learning to stay valuable**. Companies evolve, industries shift, and technology transforms the way we work—making it essential to continuously grow your skills and enhance your value. Relying solely on a company for job security is no longer viable. Instead, the key to long-term success lies in personal development, the continuous pursuit of knowledge, and the ability to adapt to new challenges.

This chapter explores the importance of ongoing learning and how it directly impacts your self-esteem, self-worth, and career trajectory. We'll examine the psychological and practical benefits of lifelong learning, how it boosts your value in the marketplace, and why it's critical to foster a mindset that seeks growth in every stage of your career.

The Corporate Myth: Job Security Doesn't Exist

The idea that working for a single company will secure your future is a myth that many have clung to for generations. It used to be that individuals could join a company and expect to stay with it for the entirety of their career. In return, they'd receive promotions, salary

There Is No Such Thing as Job Security; There Is Skill Security

increases, and eventually, a pension for retirement. But this model of corporate security has long since disappeared.

The modern economy is characterized by **constant change**. Entire industries rise and fall within a decade. Companies that were once stable giants are now struggling to stay afloat, disrupted by technology or shifts in consumer demand. A report by the World Economic Forum (WEF) predicts that automation and digital transformation will displace 85 million jobs by 2025, even as 97 million new roles are created. While opportunities continue to grow, it's clear that the skills needed to thrive in these new roles will be vastly different from those required today.

For example, consider industries like retail, manufacturing, or even IT—where automation, artificial intelligence, and machine learning are already replacing roles that were once considered stable. To remain competitive, professionals in these fields must not only keep up with new technologies but also continuously improve their skill sets to match changing job requirements.

Lifelong Learning as a Career Necessity

If job security is no longer a given, the only real security lies in **your ability to learn and adapt**. Lifelong learning is no longer optional—it's essential for survival in the workforce. Whether you're learning a new technology, adopting a new way of thinking, or developing leadership

There Is No Such Thing as Job Security; There Is Skill Security

skills, continuous learning enables you to stay ahead of the curve.

Research from the **U.S. Bureau of Labor Statistics** shows that workers who actively engage in professional development and continuous learning earn higher salaries and are more likely to be promoted than those who do not. This makes sense: companies are always seeking employees who bring more value to the table, and those who actively upskill are seen as assets, rather than liabilities.

One key advantage of continuous learning is that it directly impacts your **self-esteem** and **self-worth**. When you invest in new knowledge and skills, you increase your confidence in your abilities. This boost in self-esteem translates to greater performance at work, better job satisfaction, and an enhanced reputation among your peers and supervisors.

Boosting Self-Worth Through Continuous Learning

Developing new skills is more than just a career requirement—it's a significant way to **enhance your self-identity**. When you take the time to learn something new, you're not just adding to your resume; you're also building your sense of self-worth. Every skill you acquire becomes a tangible reminder of your ability to grow, adapt, and succeed.

There Is No Such Thing as Job Security; There Is Skill Security

According to a study by **Stanford psychologist Carol Dweck**, individuals with a "growth mindset"—the belief that talents and intelligence can be developed through hard work and learning—are more likely to succeed in their careers. Dweck's research shows that those who embrace lifelong learning tend to be more resilient in the face of challenges, more motivated to achieve their goals, and more likely to seek out feedback and new opportunities.

Building skills over time also helps to define and solidify your **professional identity**. The more you learn, the more you begin to see yourself as a competent, capable individual who can take on any challenge. This shift in identity has a powerful impact on your overall confidence, making you more likely to pursue leadership roles, collaborate with others, and innovate within your organization.

Adding Value to Your Organization

One of the most significant benefits of continuous learning is that it allows you to **add more value** to your organization. Every new skill you develop or concept you master becomes a resource you can use to solve problems, improve processes, and drive results for your company.

Employers highly value employees who proactively seek out ways to improve themselves and their work. According to the **Harvard Business Review**, companies are more

There Is No Such Thing as Job Security; There Is Skill Security

likely to promote and retain employees who demonstrate a commitment to lifelong learning, especially in leadership roles. In fact, the same report shows that organizations with a learning culture are 92% more likely to innovate, 52% more productive, and 17% more profitable than companies that don't prioritize learning.

By constantly adding value, you become indispensable to your organization. Instead of fearing job insecurity, you become the person everyone relies on for creative solutions and innovative approaches. Your role shifts from being merely functional to being vital for the company's success.

The Psychological Benefits of Lifelong Learning

Learning continuously not only improves your professional standing but also has profound psychological benefits. The **British Psychological Society** found that individuals who engage in lifelong learning report higher levels of happiness, better mental health, and lower levels of stress. This is because learning helps to foster a sense of purpose, personal achievement, and self-efficacy—all of which contribute to overall well-being.

Continuous learning also stimulates the brain, keeping it active and engaged. Studies in **neuroscience** have shown that learning new skills creates new neural pathways, helping to keep your brain healthy and agile well into old

There Is No Such Thing as Job Security; There Is Skill Security

age. This is critical in a world where mental agility is as important as physical health for long-term success.

Practical Steps to Learn Continuously and Add Value

The concept of continuous learning may sound daunting, but the key is to break it down into practical steps. Here are a few actionable ways to integrate learning into your daily routine and add value to your organization:

1. **Set Learning Goals**: Start by identifying the skills or knowledge areas you want to develop. Set specific, measurable goals—whether that's learning a new programming language, improving your public speaking, or mastering a new software tool.

2. **Invest in Professional Development**: Take advantage of workshops, online courses, certifications, and seminars. Websites like Coursera, Udemy, and LinkedIn Learning offer a wide range of affordable courses that can help you develop new skills in your field.

3. **Network and Learn from Others**: Surround yourself with people who are passionate about learning. Join professional organizations, attend conferences, and actively seek mentorship from those who can offer guidance and advice. Learning from others' experiences is just as valuable as formal education.

There Is No Such Thing as Job Security; There Is Skill Security

4. **Seek Feedback and Reflect**: Regularly ask for feedback from your peers, supervisors, and clients. Use this feedback to identify areas for improvement and take concrete steps to address them. Reflection is a critical part of the learning process—consider keeping a learning journal to track your progress.

5. **Apply What You Learn**: The best way to solidify new knowledge is to apply it in real-life situations. Look for opportunities at work to use your new skills. Whether it's taking on a new project, leading a team, or offering to teach others what you've learned, practical application ensures that your knowledge becomes a valuable asset.

6. **Stay Curious and Open-Minded**: Adopt a mindset of curiosity and openness to new ideas. Be willing to explore areas outside of your immediate expertise and take risks. Often, the most valuable lessons come from areas that push you out of your comfort zone.

Real-Life Examples of Continuous Learning and Adding Value

The concept of continuous learning is not just theoretical—it's something that countless professionals practice successfully in their careers. For example, **Elon Musk** famously taught himself rocket science through books and

There Is No Such Thing as Job Security; There Is Skill Security

discussions with experts, enabling him to launch SpaceX. Musk's ability to continuously learn and adapt to new industries—ranging from electric vehicles to space exploration—has made him one of the most innovative leaders of our time.

Another example is **Satya Nadella**, the CEO of Microsoft, who transformed the company by fostering a culture of continuous learning and innovation. Under Nadella's leadership, Microsoft shifted its focus from traditional software development to cloud computing and AI, positioning the company as a leader in the tech industry. Nadella has emphasized the importance of a "learn-it-all" mindset, as opposed to a "know-it-all" mindset, which encourages employees to prioritize learning and growth.

The Long-Term Impact of Learning on Your Career

The long-term impact of continuous learning cannot be overstated. As industries change, those who prioritize learning will be the ones who rise to the top. The ability to stay adaptable and relevant in a constantly changing job market gives you the power to shape your own career path, rather than being at the mercy of external forces.

Research from the **Pew Research Center** shows that 87% of workers believe that continuous learning is essential for career success, with younger generations placing even more emphasis on personal development. The workforce of the

There Is No Such Thing as Job Security; There Is Skill Security

future will belong to those who are willing to learn, adapt, and grow.

In fact, a report by **McKinsey & Company** suggests that employees will need to spend at least 30-40% of their time on learning and development by 2030 to keep up with technological changes and evolving job demands. This makes continuous learning not just a recommendation, but a requirement for long-term career security and success.

Conclusion: Commit to Learning, Commit to Your Future

In a world where job security isIn a world where job security is becoming less reliable, the true foundation of long-term career success lies in continuous learning. By committing to lifelong learning, you ensure that your value in the marketplace continually grows, even as industries and technologies shift. The more you learn, the more confident and adaptable you become, enhancing your self-esteem, self-worth, and professional identity.

Continuous learning offers numerous benefits, both tangible and intangible. It allows you to **stay competitive**, providing you with the knowledge and skills necessary to meet the ever-changing demands of your field. Whether it's staying current with technological advances, understanding new market trends, or developing leadership and communication skills, learning helps you adapt to external

There Is No Such Thing as Job Security; There Is Skill Security

changes rather than being left behind. A 2019 report by LinkedIn found that 94% of employees would stay longer at a company that invested in their learning, demonstrating the strong connection between learning opportunities and job satisfaction.

On a personal level, **continuous learning enhances self-worth**. When you acquire new skills, you boost your confidence, which translates into better job performance, improved relationships, and a greater sense of personal fulfillment. Each new skill or knowledge area mastered serves as a building block in your self-identity, reinforcing your ability to take on challenges, solve problems, and make meaningful contributions.

Why Continuous Learning is Non-Negotiable in a Rapidly Changing World

The rapid pace of technological advancements, automation, and digital transformation is creating both challenges and opportunities in the job market. A report from the **World Economic Forum** estimates that by 2025, 50% of all employees will need reskilling due to the rise of AI, machine learning, and other emerging technologies. The employees who thrive in this environment will be those who embrace continuous learning as a way of life.

Consider the example of the **IT industry**: The coding languages and software systems that were widely used a

There Is No Such Thing as Job Security; There Is Skill Security

decade ago have evolved or been replaced. Developers who rested on their laurels, relying solely on the skills they acquired early in their careers, now find themselves struggling to keep up. Those who consistently learn new programming languages, tools, and systems, however, remain valuable and employable, even in the face of industry upheavals.

Similarly, in **healthcare**, advances in medical technology and treatment methods are transforming the field. Medical professionals must continuously stay updated with the latest research, techniques, and tools to provide the best care possible. Those who commit to learning are not just staying afloat—they are excelling, leading to career advancement and increased job satisfaction.

The Power of Self-Esteem and Confidence Through Learning

Every time you learn a new skill or deepen your knowledge in an area, you are reinforcing the idea that you are capable, adaptable, and valuable. This boost in **self-esteem** is crucial for career longevity. Confidence is infectious; when you believe in your abilities, others—whether they are colleagues, clients, or supervisors—believe in you too.

A study published in the **Journal of Applied Psychology** found that individuals who engage in continuous learning report higher levels of job satisfaction and lower levels of

There Is No Such Thing as Job Security; There Is Skill Security

burnout. This is because learning fosters a sense of achievement and progress. When you're constantly improving yourself, you feel more in control of your career path, which in turn reduces stress and anxiety related to job security.

How Learning Creates Opportunities for Advancement

When you take the initiative to learn new skills, you position yourself for new opportunities. Whether that's a promotion within your current organization or an exciting new role at a different company, your commitment to growth is what sets you apart from your peers.

A 2020 report by **Deloitte Insights** highlighted that organizations are increasingly looking for employees who are versatile and have a wide range of skills. Employees who are capable of stepping into different roles, leading cross-functional teams, or adapting to new challenges are seen as invaluable assets. Continuous learning allows you to build this versatility, making you more attractive to employers and more likely to secure roles that offer greater responsibility, higher pay, and increased job satisfaction.

Developing a Growth Mindset

Central to the idea of continuous learning is the concept of a **growth mindset**. A term coined by Stanford psychologist **Carol Dweck**, a growth mindset refers to the belief that abilities and intelligence can be developed through hard

There Is No Such Thing as Job Security; There Is Skill Security

work, dedication, and a love of learning. People with a growth mindset view challenges as opportunities for growth, and they aren't afraid to make mistakes because they see failure as a stepping stone to success.

When you adopt a growth mindset, you stop viewing your skills as fixed or limited. Instead, you start to see yourself as a work in progress, always capable of improving and expanding your abilities. This mindset is crucial in today's job market, where adaptability is more valuable than ever.

Dweck's research has shown that people with a growth mindset are more likely to take risks, seek feedback, and pursue difficult tasks—traits that are associated with greater career success. They are also less likely to experience burnout because they view challenges as an integral part of the learning process, rather than as a threat to their self-worth.

Learning Builds Self-Identity and Purpose

Your career is not just about what you do for a living—it's about who you are and the impact you make. **Lifelong learning helps shape your self-identity**, reinforcing the idea that you are a person who grows, evolves, and contributes meaningfully to your field.

The more you learn, the more you refine your sense of purpose. You begin to see how your work fits into the bigger picture, and how your unique skills and knowledge

There Is No Such Thing as Job Security; There Is Skill Security

can make a difference. This sense of purpose is a powerful motivator, driving you to seek out new challenges and strive for excellence.

According to a study by **Yale University**, people who view their work as a calling, rather than just a job, report higher levels of career satisfaction and overall well-being. Continuous learning is a key component of finding and fulfilling your calling. It allows you to stay engaged, curious, and excited about your work—qualities that make for a fulfilling career and a meaningful life.

Adapting to Market Changes Through Learning

The rapid pace of market changes and technological advancements means that what is relevant today may be obsolete tomorrow. Industries are being disrupted by **automation, artificial intelligence**, and **digital transformation**, forcing professionals to adapt or risk becoming irrelevant. Learning continuously enables you to stay relevant in a world that is constantly evolving.

The **World Economic Forum's Future of Jobs Report** highlights that 94% of business leaders expect employees to pick up new skills on the job. This statistic underscores the need for individuals to take responsibility for their own learning. Whether it's mastering new software, understanding data analytics, or improving soft skills like

There Is No Such Thing as Job Security; There Is Skill Security

leadership and communication, the ability to learn quickly and efficiently is now a necessity in every field.

Practical Strategies for Continuous Learning

Now that we've established the importance of continuous learning, how can you make it a regular part of your career development? Here are a few practical strategies to help you integrate learning into your daily routine:

1. **Take Online Courses**: Platforms like Coursera, Udemy, and LinkedIn Learning offer a wide range of courses on topics ranging from technology to leadership. Set aside time each week to enroll in courses that align with your career goals.

2. **Join Professional Networks**: Engage with industry-specific networks and communities. Attend conferences, webinars, or networking events to learn from peers and stay updated on the latest trends in your field.

3. **Read Books and Journals**: Make reading a habit. Whether it's industry journals, business books, or biographies of successful people, reading helps you gain new perspectives and insights that can inform your career decisions.

4. **Seek Mentorship**: Learning from others is one of the most effective ways to grow. Seek out mentors

There Is No Such Thing as Job Security; There Is Skill Security

who can provide guidance, share their experiences, and offer valuable feedback on your career progress.

5. **Apply What You Learn**: Learning is most effective when you put it into practice. Look for opportunities within your current role to apply the skills you've learned. Whether it's leading a new project, improving a process, or mentoring others, practical application reinforces your knowledge and makes it more meaningful.

Conclusion: The Journey of Continuous Learning

In an unpredictable world where industries are constantly evolving, continuous learning is your greatest asset. It not only enhances your professional capabilities but also boosts your self-esteem, reinforces your self-identity, and helps you find meaning in your work. By committing to lifelong learning, you secure your value in the marketplace and set yourself up for long-term success—no matter how much the world around you changes.

In the end, learning is not just a career strategy—it's a way of life. It's about constantly seeking to improve, grow, and add value to the world around you. So, embrace the journey of continuous learning, and you'll find that not only do you remain relevant, but you also thrive in a world of constant change.

There Is No Such Thing as Job Security; There Is Skill Security

**There Is No Such Thing as Job Security;
There Is Skill Security**

Chapter 4: Work for Yourself, Not Just the Company

In the fast-changing landscape of today's corporate world, one principle becomes increasingly critical: **your work is ultimately an investment in yourself, not just the company you work for**. While loyalty to your employer is important, it's equally important to understand that your career and your skills are your own. By adopting a mindset where you're working for yourself, you ensure that you remain adaptable, relevant, and valuable—no matter where your career takes you.

This chapter explores how focusing on personal growth, skill development, and self-investment can boost your self-esteem, self-worth, and career longevity. It also emphasizes the importance of staying adaptable and resilient in the face of change, ensuring that you're always prepared for the next step in your professional journey.

The Shift in Career Ownership: Working for Yourself

Historically, people often believed that their employer would provide job security, promotions, and retirement benefits. In return, they would remain loyal to the company for decades. However, that landscape has dramatically shifted. According to a 2020 report by **Gallup**, only 12% of employees feel that job security is a strong motivator for

There Is No Such Thing as Job Security; There Is Skill Security

their long-term career choices. The rapid evolution of industries, technology, and market demands means that today's workers must take ownership of their career trajectory.

The notion of working "for yourself" doesn't mean being self-employed or starting your own business—though that is one path. It means recognizing that your skills, knowledge, and development are assets that belong to you, not your employer. Your work should be seen as an investment in yourself: every project, every skill learned, every experience gained adds value to **you**, not just your company.

The key here is to view your career as a series of building blocks. Each position you take, each skill you develop, is not just a contribution to the organization but also a way to improve your **self-worth** and **self-value**. When you start seeing your work this way, you become proactive about your development, always seeking out opportunities to learn, grow, and improve.

Building Self-Worth Through Your Work

One of the most empowering aspects of adopting the mindset of working for yourself is the **boost in self-worth** it provides. When you realize that every task you complete and every skill you acquire is an investment in yourself, it transforms the way you approach your work. You stop

There Is No Such Thing as Job Security; There Is Skill Security

viewing your job as a series of tasks to be completed for someone else's benefit, and you start seeing it as a way to increase your value in the marketplace.

This shift is backed by psychological research. A study published in the **Journal of Occupational and Organizational Psychology** found that individuals who feel in control of their professional development experience higher levels of job satisfaction and self-esteem. When you work for yourself, you take ownership of your career, and this ownership increases your sense of agency and confidence. You're no longer passively waiting for promotions or recognition—you're actively building your career on your terms.

Consider the long-term benefits: when you approach your career with a mindset of self-investment, you continuously look for ways to improve, challenge yourself, and take on new responsibilities. This constant growth not only enhances your professional abilities but also shapes your **self-identity**. You become someone who is adaptable, resilient, and always prepared for the next opportunity.

The Importance of Adaptability

In a world where companies rise and fall, industries transform, and technology evolves, the ability to **adapt** is one of the most critical skills you can develop. No matter how stable your current position may seem, external forces

There Is No Such Thing as Job Security; There Is Skill Security

can disrupt your career overnight. The COVID-19 pandemic, for example, reshaped industries worldwide, forcing millions of people to either adapt or be left behind. Those who thrived during this period were not necessarily the most skilled or knowledgeable—but they were the most adaptable.

According to a **McKinsey & Company** report, 50% of jobs today are at risk of being automated or drastically changed by technology in the next decade. This means that even those in traditionally "secure" fields must be prepared to pivot, learn new skills, and embrace new ways of working. Adaptability is the key to surviving and thriving in this new professional landscape.

But how do you become adaptable? The answer lies in continuous learning and **personal development**. By consistently seeking out new knowledge, taking on diverse projects, and stepping outside your comfort zone, you develop a mindset of growth that allows you to adjust to new circumstances with ease. In fact, a **Harvard Business Review** study found that employees who proactively embrace change and continuously learn are 40% more likely to be promoted and 45% more likely to experience long-term career success.

Continuous Learning: Investing in Yourself

There Is No Such Thing as Job Security; There Is Skill Security

At the heart of working for yourself is the concept of **continuous learning**. When you view your work as an investment in yourself, you naturally become more focused on acquiring new skills and knowledge. Whether it's learning a new software program, taking leadership courses, or developing emotional intelligence, continuous learning is essential for maintaining your value in an ever-changing job market.

A report by the **World Economic Forum** found that by 2025, nearly half of all workers will need reskilling as technology and market demands evolve. The same report emphasizes that employees who prioritize learning will be in a much stronger position to remain employable and competitive.

But continuous learning isn't just about staying relevant—it's also about **boosting your self-esteem**. Every new skill you learn becomes a source of pride and accomplishment. This sense of achievement reinforces your belief in your abilities and your potential, leading to greater job satisfaction and career success.

In my own career, continuous learning has been a cornerstone of my growth. I've always sought out opportunities to learn—whether it was mastering new programming languages, attending workshops on leadership, or reading books on emotional intelligence. Each new skill I acquired didn't just make me a better

There Is No Such Thing as Job Security; There Is Skill Security

employee—it made me a more valuable individual, capable of adapting to new challenges and seizing new opportunities.

Personal Branding: Your Career is Your Business

One of the most empowering aspects of working for yourself is the idea of **personal branding**. In today's digital age, everyone has a brand—whether they realize it or not. Your personal brand is how you present yourself to the world, how you communicate your value, and how others perceive you.

When you work for yourself, you take control of your personal brand. You no longer rely on your company's reputation to define you. Instead, you focus on building your own reputation based on your skills, values, and contributions. This shift in mindset empowers you to take ownership of your career and ensures that you're always in demand, regardless of where you work.

A **LinkedIn survey** found that professionals with a strong personal brand are 31% more likely to receive job offers and 44% more likely to be promoted. This is because personal branding allows you to stand out in a crowded marketplace. When employers and clients see you as someone who consistently adds value and demonstrates expertise, they are more likely to seek you out for new opportunities.

There Is No Such Thing as Job Security; There Is Skill Security

Building a personal brand doesn't happen overnight, but it's a critical investment in your future. Start by identifying your unique strengths, passions, and values. What sets you apart from others in your field? How do you want to be perceived by your colleagues, clients, and potential employers? Once you've defined your brand, you can begin to actively cultivate it through networking, content creation, and thought leadership.

Self-Esteem and Self-Worth: The Benefits of Taking Ownership

One of the most powerful effects of working for yourself is the impact it has on your **self-esteem** and **self-worth**. When you take control of your career and view every task, project, and skill as an investment in yourself, you naturally begin to see yourself in a more positive light. You stop relying on external validation from your employer or colleagues and start valuing yourself based on your own achievements and progress.

This boost in self-esteem is backed by psychological research. A study by the **University of California, Berkeley** found that individuals who take ownership of their professional development experience higher levels of job satisfaction and self-confidence. When you believe in your ability to shape your own career, you become more resilient in the face of challenges and more motivated to pursue new opportunities.

There Is No Such Thing as Job Security; There Is Skill Security

In my own experience, taking ownership of my career has been one of the most empowering decisions I've made. Early in my career, I realized that no company could provide me with long-term security. Instead of relying on promotions or raises to validate my worth, I focused on building my skills, expanding my knowledge, and taking on projects that challenged me. This shift in mindset allowed me to develop a sense of self-worth that wasn't tied to any specific job or title—it was rooted in my ability to grow, adapt, and succeed.

Resilience: Thriving in Uncertainty

One of the greatest advantages of working for yourself is that it builds **resilience**. When you view your career as your own business, you become less vulnerable to the ups and downs of the corporate world. Whether it's an economic downturn, a company restructuring, or a shift in industry trends, you're better equipped to navigate uncertainty because you've invested in yourself.

Resilience is not just about surviving difficult times—it's about thriving in them. A report by the **American Psychological Association** found that individuals who are resilient in the face of adversity are more likely to experience career success and personal fulfillment. This is because resilience allows you to bounce back from setbacks, learn from failures, and approach challenges with a growth mindset.

There Is No Such Thing as Job Security; There Is Skill Security

When you work for yourself, you're constantly developing the skills and mindset needed to adapt to new circumstances. You're not afraid of change, because you've built a foundation of knowledge, experience, and self-confidence that allows you to navigate any situation with confidence.

****The Psychological Impact of Self-Invest####
Resilience: Thriving in Uncertainty**

One of the greatest advantages of working for yourself is that it builds **resilience**. When you view your career as your own business, you become less vulnerable to the ups and downs of the corporate world. Whether it's an economic downturn, a company restructuring, or a shift in industry trends, you're better equipped to navigate uncertainty because you've invested in yourself.

Resilience is not just about surviving difficult times—it's about thriving in them. A report by the **American Psychological Association** found that individuals who are resilient in the face of adversity are more likely to experience career success and personal fulfillment. This is because resilience allows you to bounce back from setbacks, learn from failures, and approach challenges with a growth mindset.

When you work for yourself, you're constantly developing the skills and mindset needed to adapt to new

There Is No Such Thing as Job Security; There Is Skill Security

circumstances. You're not afraid of change, because you've built a foundation of knowledge, experience, and self-confidence that allows you to navigate any situation with confidence.

The Psychological Impact of Self-Investment

When you begin to view your work as an investment in yourself, you're likely to experience a profound psychological shift. Instead of feeling like a cog in a corporate machine, you start to see your work as a means of personal growth and development. This shift can lead to increased job satisfaction, greater motivation, and a stronger sense of purpose.

Studies have shown that people who feel a sense of autonomy and ownership over their work are more engaged and more productive. A report by **Gallup** found that employees who feel empowered to take control of their professional development are 67% more engaged in their work and 70% more likely to remain with their company long-term. This sense of ownership fosters a mindset of growth and resilience, both of which are critical for long-term career success.

Building a Portfolio of Skills

When you work for yourself, you're not just doing a job—you're building a portfolio of skills and experiences that will serve you throughout your career. Every new project,

There Is No Such Thing as Job Security; There Is Skill Security

every new challenge, and every new skill you acquire becomes part of your personal portfolio, increasing your value in the marketplace.

Think of your career as a series of investments. Each task you complete, each skill you develop, is an investment in your future. By building a diverse portfolio of skills, you make yourself more adaptable and more valuable. You're not just relying on one job or one set of skills to carry you through your career—you're constantly adding new tools to your toolkit, making you more resilient and more capable of handling whatever comes your way.

The Power of Self-Identity

Perhaps the most significant benefit of working for yourself is the impact it has on your **self-identity**. When you take ownership of your career, you begin to see yourself as more than just an employee—you see yourself as a valuable asset, a lifelong learner, and someone capable of achieving great things.

This shift in self-identity is incredibly powerful. It allows you to approach your work with confidence and a sense of purpose. You're no longer working to meet someone else's expectations—you're working to fulfill your own potential.

According to a study by the **University of California, Berkeley**, individuals with a strong sense of self-identity are more likely to experience career success and personal

There Is No Such Thing as Job Security; There Is Skill Security

fulfillment. This is because they approach their work with a sense of purpose and motivation, which leads to greater engagement and a willingness to take on new challenges.

The Urgency of Adaptability in a Changing World

In today's world, the ability to adapt has never been more critical. As industries continue to evolve, companies are looking for employees who are not only skilled but also adaptable. The rise of automation, artificial intelligence, and remote work has transformed the way we do business, and those who fail to adapt risk being left behind.

A report by **Deloitte** found that 94% of business leaders believe that the most important skill for the future workforce is adaptability. This means that workers who are willing to learn new skills, embrace new technologies, and adapt to changing circumstances will be in the highest demand.

The ability to adapt is not just about survival—it's about thriving in a constantly changing world. By viewing your work as an investment in yourself, you're better equipped to adapt to new challenges and opportunities. You're not tied to a specific job or industry—you have the skills and mindset to succeed in any environment.

Conclusion: Work for Yourself, Build Your Future

There Is No Such Thing as Job Security; There Is Skill Security

In a world where job security is no longer guaranteed, the only true security lies in your ability to invest in yourself. By adopting the mindset of working for yourself, you take control of your career and your future. Every task you complete, every skill you learn, and every project you take on becomes part of your personal portfolio, increasing your value and making you more adaptable to change.

Working for yourself is not just about surviving in today's job market—it's about thriving. It's about building a career that is resilient, adaptable, and always growing. It's about taking ownership of your professional development and seeing your work as an investment in your future.

By focusing on continuous learning, developing a growth mindset, and taking control of your personal brand, you ensure that you'll always be in demand, no matter where your career takes you. The journey of working for yourself is not an easy one, but it is the most rewarding path to long-term career success and personal fulfillment.

So, as you move forward in your career, remember this: **you're not just working for a company—you're working for yourself**. Every day is an opportunity to invest in your skills, your knowledge, and your future. And with the right mindset, the possibilities are endless.

**There Is No Such Thing as Job Security;
There Is Skill Security**

Chapter 5: AI and The Transparency of Productivity

The dawn of artificial intelligence (AI) has not only transformed industries but also brought a new level of transparency to the workplace. As AI becomes more integrated into our daily operations, it exposes inefficiencies, identifies gaps in productivity, and tracks individual contributions with greater precision than ever before. In this chapter, we explore how AI has created a new paradigm of accountability in the workplace, focusing on honesty, productivity, and the need for consistent, meaningful contributions.

This chapter will also examine how AI impacts self-worth, self-identity, and self-esteem, as well as the necessity of adapting to this new reality. The world of work is changing rapidly, and it is essential to embrace AI as a tool to not only enhance productivity but also to ensure that every action and contribution you make is visible and valued.

The Age of AI: A Shift in Productivity and Accountability

AI has changed the way we approach work by providing real-time insights into efficiency, productivity, and performance. Whether through automated systems that track work processes, machine learning algorithms that

There Is No Such Thing as Job Security; There Is Skill Security

optimize tasks, or AI-driven analytics that measure employee output, the new landscape of work is one of transparency. No longer can inefficiencies, procrastination, or lack of productivity go unnoticed.

According to a 2021 study by **McKinsey & Company**, AI adoption in the workplace has increased by over 60% since 2017, and this trend is only accelerating. AI tools have proven their ability to streamline processes, automate repetitive tasks, and enhance decision-making by providing data-driven insights. However, along with these benefits comes a higher level of visibility—AI tools expose inefficiencies and inconsistencies that might have previously gone unnoticed.

In an AI-driven workplace, every action is measurable, every delay is trackable, and every inefficiency is visible. This level of transparency pushes employees to stay productive and accountable for their daily contributions. Whether you're in a leadership role or an entry-level position, AI will evaluate your work based on concrete metrics, such as output, quality, and adherence to deadlines.

Productivity in the Age of AI: Why Daily Contributions Matter

The advent of AI has also shifted the way we think about productivity. Rather than measuring success by hours spent at a desk or the number of tasks completed, productivity is

There Is No Such Thing as Job Security; There Is Skill Security

now measured by value-added contributions. AI tools enable companies to track the **real impact** of your work, ensuring that your output directly aligns with organizational goals and contributes to overall success.

The importance of making meaningful daily contributions cannot be overstated in the age of AI. Because AI can identify inefficiencies with ease, it holds employees accountable not just for the quantity of work they produce, but also for the quality and relevance of that work. The days of "looking busy" without adding tangible value are over.

For example, **Gartner** predicts that by 2025, 75% of organizations will implement AI-based tools to assess workforce productivity, creating an environment where consistent, high-quality contributions are required for professional advancement. This means that the key to thriving in this AI-dominated world is to focus on creating value every single day. Employees must now be proactive, efficient, and innovative to stand out in an environment where performance is constantly monitored.

Self-Esteem and Self-Worth in an AI-Driven Workplace

One of the most significant challenges of working in an AI-driven world is the potential impact on **self-esteem** and **self-worth**. In the past, employees could sometimes take pride in simply maintaining a stable job or performing

There Is No Such Thing as Job Security; There Is Skill Security

routine tasks. However, as AI takes over mundane tasks and exposes inefficiencies, employees may feel threatened, fearing that their contributions are not valued or that they could be easily replaced.

It's important to understand that while AI can perform certain functions more efficiently than humans, it cannot replace the **human touch**—creativity, emotional intelligence, leadership, and strategic thinking remain areas where humans excel. In fact, the rise of AI highlights the importance of **soft skills**, such as communication, adaptability, and emotional intelligence.

According to a report by the **World Economic Forum**, skills like critical thinking, problem-solving, and creativity are becoming more valuable than ever in the AI age. The report states that while automation will replace certain tasks, it will also create new opportunities for individuals who possess these uniquely human abilities.

To thrive in an AI-driven environment, you must focus on the aspects of your work that machines cannot replicate—creativity, leadership, relationship-building, and innovation. By honing these skills, you reinforce your self-worth and ensure that your contributions remain indispensable.

Honesty and Integrity: The Cornerstones of Success in the Age of AI

There Is No Such Thing as Job Security; There Is Skill Security

In an environment where AI tracks every move and productivity is transparent, **honesty** and **integrity** become even more crucial. Faking productivity, cutting corners, or engaging in unethical behavior is easily exposed in the world of AI. AI systems can analyze patterns, detect anomalies, and identify discrepancies in data, making it much harder to conceal inefficiencies or dishonesty.

The increased transparency brought by AI demands a higher level of **accountability** and **ethical behavior** from employees. A study conducted by **Accenture** revealed that companies that adopt AI-driven transparency and accountability measures report higher levels of trust and employee engagement. This suggests that transparency not only benefits organizations but also fosters a more positive work environment where trust and honesty are prioritized.

In the AI age, ethical behavior is not just about following the rules—it's about consistently doing the right thing, even when no one is watching. AI may track your output, but your integrity is measured by your actions, decisions, and how you treat others. Building a reputation for honesty and integrity ensures that you remain a trusted and valued member of your organization, regardless of the changes brought about by AI.

The Power of Transparency: A Double-Edged Sword

There Is No Such Thing as Job Security; There Is Skill Security

While the transparency created by AI has its benefits, it can also create challenges for employees who struggle with the constant scrutiny. Knowing that every task, every interaction, and every decision is being monitored can feel overwhelming, leading to anxiety or stress. However, it's essential to view transparency as an opportunity for growth and improvement, rather than as a threat.

Transparency allows you to **see your strengths and weaknesses** clearly, giving you the chance to improve and grow. Instead of fearing AI's ability to expose inefficiencies, use it to your advantage. Leverage the data provided by AI to identify areas where you can improve, and take proactive steps to enhance your skills and productivity.

A study by **PwC** showed that companies with high levels of workplace transparency are more likely to foster a culture of continuous learning and development. Employees in transparent environments are encouraged to seek feedback, improve their skills, and take ownership of their development. This culture of openness and growth is essential for thriving in an AI-driven workplace.

Adapting to AI: Embrace the Change, Don't Resist It

One of the most important lessons of working in an AI-driven environment is the need for **adaptability**. AI is here to stay, and resisting its influence is futile. Instead,

There Is No Such Thing as Job Security; There Is Skill Security

employees must learn to embrace AI as a tool for enhancing productivity, creativity, and decision-making.

Adaptability in the AI age means continuously upgrading your skills, staying curious about new technologies, and being open to change. It also means accepting that your work will be more visible and measurable than ever before—and using this visibility as motivation to improve.

A report by **Deloitte** found that 90% of executives believe that adaptability is one of the most important skills for the future workforce. Those who can adapt to AI, integrate it into their daily work, and use it to improve productivity will thrive. Conversely, those who resist change or fail to keep up with technological advancements will struggle to remain relevant.

How AI Enhances Self-Identity and Professional Growth

The integration of AI into the workplace has the potential to enhance your **self-identity** by encouraging you to focus on the unique skills and talents that set you apart from machines. As AI takes over repetitive and mundane tasks, it frees up time for employees to focus on higher-level work—work that requires creativity, problem-solving, and innovation.

By allowing AI to handle routine tasks, you can focus on projects that align with your passions and strengths. This

There Is No Such Thing as Job Security; There Is Skill Security

shift in focus not only increases job satisfaction but also helps you refine your **professional identity**. You are no longer defined by the routine tasks you complete, but by the meaningful contributions you make to the organization's success.

According to a study by the **MIT Sloan School of Management**, employees who work in AI-enhanced environments report higher levels of job satisfaction and fulfillment. This is because AI allows them to focus on work that is more aligned with their skills and interests, leading to greater engagement and a stronger sense of purpose.

The Future of Work: Collaboration Between Humans and AI

As AI continues to evolve, the future of work will be defined by **collaboration between humans and machines**. Rather than viewing AI as a threat, it's important to see it as a partner that enhances your abilities and helps you achieve greater levels of productivity and success.

The most successful professionals in the AI age will be those who can seamlessly integrate AI into their work, leveraging its capabilities to enhance their creativity, decision-making, and problem-solving. By working alongside AI, you can maximize your productivity and

There Is No Such Thing as Job Security; There Is Skill Security

ensure that your contributions remain relevant and valuable.

In fact, the **World Economic Forum** predicts that by 2025, the most successful organizations will be those that foster a culture of collaboration between humans and AI. These organizations will not only achieve higher levels of innovation and efficiency but also create a more fulfilling and engaging work environment for their employees.

Conclusion: Honesty, Productivity, and Transparency in the AI Age

As AI continues to transform the workplace, it's essential to adapt to the new reality of **transparency and accountability**. AI exposes inefficiencies, tracks productivity, and holds employees accountable for their daily contributions.AI is revolutionizing the workplace, bringing unparalleled transparency to how we measure productivity, performance, and honesty. It exposes inefficiencies, highlights daily contributions, and holds individuals accountable. In the AI age, it's critical to focus on genuine productivity, ethical behavior, and making a positive impact daily.

Employees must adapt, learning to integrate AI as a tool that enhances—not replaces—human creativity, emotional intelligence, and decision-making. The constant visibility AI provides should be embraced as an opportunity for self-

There Is No Such Thing as Job Security; There Is Skill Security

improvement and growth, elevating self-worth, and creating a resilient, adaptable mindset.

AI Exposes Inefficiencies and Encourages Honesty

Artificial intelligence tracks and measures every aspect of workplace productivity. Whether it's automating tasks, monitoring work patterns, or analyzing data, AI systems can easily detect inefficiencies and identify underperformance. A study by **McKinsey** indicates that AI can increase business productivity by 40% in certain industries, but it also holds individuals accountable for contributing meaningfully to their organization. No longer can employees hide behind busywork or unproductive habits—AI brings honesty and transparency to the forefront of daily work.

Daily Contributions Matter More Than Ever

Because AI tracks work in real-time, **consistent daily contributions** are more critical than ever before. In the past, employees might have relied on occasional bursts of productivity to meet deadlines. Now, AI systems can measure productivity continuously, creating an environment where adding value every day is necessary. According to **Gartner**, by 2025, most organizations will rely on AI-based tools to measure and monitor workforce contributions.

There Is No Such Thing as Job Security; There Is Skill Security

To stay competitive, employees must learn to focus on making high-quality, meaningful contributions every day. Rather than seeing this transparency as a threat, use it as motivation to perform at your best and continually improve your output. By embracing daily productivity as a habit, you build trust, improve your value to the organization, and prepare yourself for future challenges.

The Psychological Impact of AI on Self-Worth

While AI offers incredible benefits to workplace efficiency, it also raises concerns about the psychological impact on employees. Many workers worry that AI could replace their jobs or that the increased monitoring could lead to stress and anxiety. These concerns are valid, but they overlook an essential point: **AI cannot replace human creativity, leadership, or emotional intelligence**.

A report by the **World Economic Forum** emphasizes that while AI will automate many repetitive tasks, it will also create new opportunities for individuals who excel in areas where machines cannot. Skills like creativity, problem-solving, emotional intelligence, and communication are more valuable than ever in the AI age. These skills, often referred to as "soft skills," are becoming the cornerstone of career advancement.

By focusing on developing these skills, employees can boost their self-worth and ensure that their contributions

There Is No Such Thing as Job Security; There Is Skill Security

remain indispensable, even in an AI-driven world. Instead of fearing AI, individuals should embrace it as a tool that amplifies their unique abilities and frees them from routine tasks, allowing them to focus on more meaningful work.

Honesty, Integrity, and Accountability in the AI Age

One of the most significant shifts AI brings to the workplace is the emphasis on **honesty, integrity, and accountability**. AI systems can detect patterns, anomalies, and discrepancies in data, making it nearly impossible to hide inefficiencies or unethical behavior. As transparency increases, so does the need for employees to operate with integrity and accountability.

A study by **Accenture** found that companies that implemented AI-driven transparency measures saw increased trust, engagement, and productivity among employees. This finding suggests that AI, when used effectively, can foster a more ethical and accountable workplace culture.

In the AI age, integrity is not just about following the rules—it's about consistently acting in ways that reflect honesty and transparency. Employees who demonstrate integrity will be more trusted and valued, both by their colleagues and their employers.

The Power of Adaptability

There Is No Such Thing as Job Security; There Is Skill Security

As AI continues to transform industries, **adaptability** becomes a critical skill for long-term career success. The ability to adapt to new technologies, new roles, and new ways of working will separate those who thrive from those who struggle. According to **Deloitte**, 94% of business leaders believe that adaptability is one of the most important skills for the future workforce.

AI offers employees the tools to enhance their productivity, but those who refuse to embrace these tools will find themselves falling behind. The most successful professionals will be those who can learn to work alongside AI, integrating it into their workflows and using it to their advantage. Adaptability also requires a willingness to continuously learn and grow. As AI evolves, so too must your skills and mindset.

AI as a Tool for Growth and Development

While AI tracks productivity and exposes inefficiencies, it also offers immense potential for **personal and professional growth**. The data provided by AI allows you to identify areas where you can improve and grow. Rather than fearing AI's ability to monitor your work, use it to gain insights into your strengths and weaknesses.

Organizations that embrace AI as a tool for continuous learning and improvement are more likely to foster a culture of growth. Employees can leverage AI to enhance

There Is No Such Thing as Job Security; There Is Skill Security

their skills, seek feedback, and take ownership of their development. By using AI to track your progress, you can set clear goals, measure your achievements, and identify areas for further growth.

Embracing AI: Collaboration Between Humans and Machines

The future of work lies in the **collaboration between humans and AI**. Rather than replacing human workers, AI is a tool that can enhance human abilities, streamline workflows, and improve decision-making. The key to thriving in this AI-driven world is to embrace AI as a partner, rather than viewing it as a competitor.

According to the **World Economic Forum**, the most successful organizations of the future will be those that encourage collaboration between humans and AI. Employees who can integrate AI into their daily work, using it to boost productivity, creativity, and problem-solving, will be the most valuable.

By embracing AI as a tool for growth, rather than resisting it, you can position yourself as an indispensable asset in the workplace. The ability to work alongside AI will become a critical factor in determining career success in the years to come.

The Transparency of Productivity: A New Era of Accountability

There Is No Such Thing as Job Security; There Is Skill Security

As AI continues to advance, the concept of **productivity** is being redefined. In the past, productivity was often measured by the number of hours spent at work or the number of tasks completed. However, AI has introduced a new level of transparency, where productivity is measured by **value-added contributions**—the real impact of your work on the organization's success.

The transparency brought by AI holds employees accountable for their daily contributions, making it impossible to hide behind "busywork" or unproductive habits. AI tracks performance in real-time, providing organizations with data on employee efficiency, output quality, and adherence to deadlines.

For employees, this transparency creates a new level of responsibility. You must focus on consistently adding value, rather than simply meeting minimum expectations. By embracing transparency and using it as a motivator to improve, you can build a reputation as a productive, efficient, and reliable worker.

Conclusion: Honesty, Productivity, and Daily Contributions in the Age of AI

In the AI-driven workplace, transparency, productivity, and accountability are more important than ever. AI exposes inefficiencies, tracks productivity, and holds employees accountable for their daily contributions. While this may

There Is No Such Thing as Job Security; There Is Skill Security

seem daunting, it's essential to view AI as a tool for growth and improvement.

By focusing on **honesty, integrity, and daily contributions**, you can thrive in the age of AI. Embrace the transparency that AI provides, and use it as a motivator to continually improve your performance. Cultivate skills that AI cannot replace—creativity, leadership, emotional intelligence—and position yourself as an indispensable asset in the workplace.

As AI continues to evolve, those who adapt, learn, and embrace change will be the ones who succeed. By viewing AI as a partner, rather than a competitor, you can leverage its capabilities to enhance your productivity, boost your self-worth, and build a fulfilling, successful career in the modern workplace.

There Is No Such Thing as Job Security; There Is Skill Security

Chapter 6: Adaptability Is Your Greatest Asset

In today's fast-paced world, adaptability has emerged as the most critical skill for long-term success. Whether you're working in technology, healthcare, finance, or the arts, the ability to embrace change and thrive in new environments is essential. Those who resist change or cling to old ways of working often find themselves falling behind, while those who cultivate flexibility are better positioned to navigate disruptions and seize new opportunities.

This chapter will explore how adaptability boosts self-esteem, self-identity, and career growth, and it will offer practical strategies for fostering a mindset of flexibility. By embracing change and continually learning new skills, you can remain relevant and valuable in any industry, no matter how rapidly it evolves.

Why Adaptability Is the Key to Success in the Modern World

Adaptability is the cornerstone of survival in the modern workplace. The ability to adjust to changing environments, learn new technologies, and take on new challenges with confidence is a skill that transcends industries. In fact, a study by **LinkedIn Learning** found that adaptability is one

There Is No Such Thing as Job Security; There Is Skill Security

of the top soft skills employers value, with 69% of hiring managers citing it as a critical factor for success.

Industries are being disrupted faster than ever before. Automation, artificial intelligence (AI), and digital transformation have fundamentally changed how companies operate. The COVID-19 pandemic accelerated many of these changes, forcing businesses and employees to adapt to remote work, new technologies, and shifting consumer demands.

In a world where entire industries can be upended overnight, those who are adaptable will be the ones who thrive. **A report by McKinsey & Company** suggests that by 2030, more than 375 million workers will need to switch occupations or learn new skills due to automation. For professionals across industries, the ability to adapt to these shifts will determine their long-term success.

How Adaptability Impacts Self-Esteem and Self-Worth

One of the most profound benefits of adaptability is the boost it provides to your **self-esteem** and **self-worth**. When you embrace change and demonstrate your ability to learn new skills, you reinforce your belief in your capabilities. Every time you adapt to a new challenge or successfully navigate a disruption, you build confidence in your ability to handle whatever comes next.

There Is No Such Thing as Job Security; There Is Skill Security

This sense of accomplishment fosters **self-efficacy**, which refers to your belief in your ability to achieve your goals. A study published by **Harvard Business Review** found that individuals who view themselves as adaptable are more likely to pursue new opportunities, take on leadership roles, and overcome setbacks. When you know you can handle change, you're more likely to seek out challenges and push yourself outside of your comfort zone.

Adaptability also shapes your **self-identity**. By embracing change and continuously learning, you begin to see yourself as someone who is capable, resilient, and open to growth. This mindset becomes part of your identity, making you more likely to take risks and pursue opportunities that align with your goals.

The Role of Technology in Adaptability

In today's digital age, technology is a driving force behind the need for adaptability. New tools, platforms, and systems are being introduced at an unprecedented rate, and professionals across industries must keep up to stay competitive. According to the **World Economic Forum's Future of Jobs Report**, technology skills, including proficiency in AI, data analysis, and digital marketing, are among the most in-demand skills for the future workforce.

While technology can be intimidating, it's important to view it as an opportunity rather than a threat. Embracing

There Is No Such Thing as Job Security; There Is Skill Security

new technologies allows you to stay relevant and competitive, and it positions you as a leader in your field. For example, AI tools can automate repetitive tasks, giving you more time to focus on creative problem-solving and strategic thinking—areas where humans still outperform machines.

Learning new technologies is also a powerful way to boost your adaptability. Whether it's mastering a new software platform, learning to code, or staying updated on industry-specific tools, continuously upgrading your tech skills ensures that you remain valuable in a rapidly changing job market.

Practical Tips for Developing Adaptability

1. **Embrace a Growth Mindset**: Cultivating adaptability starts with adopting a growth mindset—the belief that your abilities and intelligence can be developed through hard work, learning, and persistence. When you have a growth mindset, you view challenges and setbacks as opportunities to learn and grow, rather than as threats to your competence.

A study by **Stanford University psychologist Carol Dweck** found that individuals with a growth mindset are more likely to achieve success because they are open to learning, willing to take risks, and resilient in the face of

There Is No Such Thing as Job Security; There Is Skill Security

failure. By embracing this mindset, you can view every change or disruption as a chance to improve yourself and your skills.

2. **Stay Curious and Open to Learning**: One of the best ways to cultivate adaptability is to maintain a sense of curiosity and a willingness to learn. In today's world, new skills and technologies are constantly emerging, and it's important to stay updated on industry trends. Whether it's attending workshops, taking online courses, or simply reading about new developments in your field, continuous learning ensures that you're always prepared to adapt.

Platforms like **Coursera, Udemy,** and **LinkedIn Learning** offer a wealth of resources for professionals looking to upskill. By dedicating time to learning, you can develop new competencies and stay relevant in your industry.

3. **Seek Feedback and Reflect**: Adaptability requires a willingness to reflect on your strengths and weaknesses. Regularly seeking feedback from peers, supervisors, and mentors can provide valuable insights into areas where you can improve. This feedback allows you to make adjustments and refine your skills, helping you stay agile in a rapidly changing work environment.

There Is No Such Thing as Job Security; There Is Skill Security

4. **Be Proactive About Change**: Rather than waiting for change to happen to you, be proactive about seeking out new opportunities and challenges. Volunteer for new projects, take on leadership roles, and look for ways to innovate within your organization. Being proactive about change not only demonstrates your adaptability but also positions you as a leader who can handle complex, evolving environments.

A **Deloitte study** found that employees who proactively seek out new responsibilities and challenges are 50% more likely to be promoted and 70% more likely to stay engaged in their work. By taking initiative, you can build a reputation as someone who is adaptable and capable of thriving in any situation.

5. **Practice Emotional Resilience**: Adaptability is not just about learning new skills—it's also about being emotionally resilient in the face of change. Change can be stressful, and it's important to develop coping mechanisms that allow you to stay calm and focused during periods of uncertainty.

Emotional resilience involves managing your emotions, staying positive, and finding ways to bounce back from setbacks. **Research from the American Psychological Association (APA)** shows that individuals who practice emotional resilience are better equipped to handle

There Is No Such Thing as Job Security; There Is Skill Security

workplace stress and are more likely to succeed in dynamic environments.

6. **Expand Your Network**: Building a diverse network of professionals across industries can enhance your adaptability. By surrounding yourself with people who have different perspectives, skills, and experiences, you expose yourself to new ideas and opportunities. Networking allows you to learn from others, stay informed about industry trends, and gain support during times of transition.

A **LinkedIn report** found that 85% of jobs are filled through networking, underscoring the importance of building relationships with professionals in your field. Networking not only helps you stay adaptable, but it also opens doors to new career opportunities and collaborations.

The Benefits of Adaptability: Career Growth and Job Security

Adaptability is a key factor in **career growth**. In a rapidly changing job market, those who can adapt to new roles, technologies, and challenges are more likely to advance in their careers. Employers value employees who can think critically, solve problems, and innovate in response to change.

In fact, a **Gallup survey** revealed that employees who demonstrate adaptability are 29% more likely to be

There Is No Such Thing as Job Security; There Is Skill Security

promoted within their organization. This is because adaptable employees are seen as valuable assets who can take on leadership roles and guide their teams through periods of disruption.

Adaptability also enhances **job security**. While no job is truly secure in today's world, those who are adaptable are better positioned to weather economic downturns, company restructurings, and industry shifts. By continuously learning and staying relevant, you increase your value to employers, making you less vulnerable to layoffs or job displacement.

Adapting to Industry Disruptions: A Case Study

One of the best examples of the importance of adaptability is the retail industry. Over the past decade, the rise of e-commerce has disrupted traditional brick-and-mortar retail businesses, forcing companies and employees to adapt to new technologies and consumer behaviors.

Retailers who embraced digital transformation—by launching e-commerce platforms, optimizing supply chains with AI, and enhancing the customer experience through data analytics—were able to thrive, even as competitors struggled to survive. Similarly, employees who adapted by learning digital marketing, data analysis, and customer service skills found new opportunities in the rapidly evolving retail landscape.

There Is No Such Thing as Job Security; There Is Skill Security

The COVID-19 pandemic further accelerated this shift, with consumers increasingly relying on online shopping. According to a report by **Statista**, global e-commerce sales grew by 27.6% in 2020, highlighting the need for retailers and employees to adapt to new consumer behaviors.

The lesson here is clear: industries will continue to face disruptions, and those who are adaptable will be the ones who succeed. Whether you're working in retail, healthcare, finance, or technology, adaptability is the key to staying relevant and thriving in the face of change.

The Role of AI and Automation in Adaptability

AI and automation are transforming industries across the board, and professionals must learn to adapt to these technologies to remain competitive. According to a **PwC report**, 45% of jobs in developed economies are at risk of being automated in the next two decades. However, this doesn't mean that AI will replace#### Chapter 6:
Adaptability Is Your Greatest Asset

In today's rapidly evolving workplace, adaptability is more than just a valuable skill—it's a critical asset that can make or break your career. The ability to embrace change, learn new technologies, and remain flexible amid industry disruptions ensures long-term success, no matter the challenges you face. Whether it's automation, new market

There Is No Such Thing as Job Security; There Is Skill Security

dynamics, or unexpected global events, adaptability sets apart those who thrive from those who struggle.

This chapter will dive into the reasons why adaptability is essential, how it impacts your self-esteem and self-identity, and why it's a skill that should be cultivated. We'll explore practical strategies to foster adaptability, share insights from leading studies, and highlight real-world examples of professionals who have adapted to stay relevant in their industries.

The Importance of Adaptability in a Changing World

Adaptability is more than just a reactive skill; it's a proactive mindset that prepares you for whatever challenges the workplace throws at you. As industries shift and technology advances, adaptability ensures that you're ready to meet new demands with confidence.

The workplace has changed dramatically over the past decade, and this evolution is only accelerating. A **World Economic Forum** report highlights that **half of the global workforce will need reskilling by 2025** due to the rapid rise of automation and artificial intelligence (AI). This statistic shows that being adaptable is not only helpful—it's essential for survival in the workforce.

One example of adaptability in action is the rapid shift to remote work during the COVID-19 pandemic. According to **McKinsey & Company**, 80% of executives surveyed

There Is No Such Thing as Job Security; There Is Skill Security

reported that their companies accelerated the adoption of digital solutions and remote working due to the pandemic. Professionals who could quickly adapt to new tools and ways of working thrived, while those resistant to change faced difficulties.

How Adaptability Boosts Self-Esteem and Self-Worth

Adaptability is closely linked to **self-esteem** and **self-worth**. When you navigate new challenges with ease, you reinforce your belief in your abilities, leading to a significant boost in confidence. This creates a positive feedback loop—each time you adapt to a new situation, your self-worth grows, and you become more willing to take on new challenges.

Psychological research supports this link between adaptability and self-esteem. A study published in the **Journal of Applied Psychology** found that individuals who view themselves as adaptable tend to have higher levels of job satisfaction and self-efficacy. This sense of competence encourages them to pursue new opportunities and handle changes with resilience.

Adaptability also plays a crucial role in shaping your **self-identity**. When you see yourself as someone who can handle any challenge, you naturally view change as an opportunity for growth rather than a threat. This

There Is No Such Thing as Job Security; There Is Skill Security

adaptability mindset empowers you to take on new roles, learn new skills, and expand your professional identity.

Practical Strategies to Cultivate Adaptability

1. **Embrace Continuous Learning**: The most adaptable people are lifelong learners. They understand that staying relevant in any industry means constantly acquiring new skills and knowledge. Whether it's learning a new programming language, mastering new digital tools, or staying updated on industry trends, continuous learning ensures you're always ready for the next challenge.

According to a report by **LinkedIn Learning**, 94% of employees said they would stay longer at a company that invests in their learning and development. Investing in yourself is not just about staying employable—it's also about reinforcing your self-worth.

2. **Stay Open-Minded**: A key component of adaptability is having an open mind. This means being receptive to new ideas, approaches, and technologies, even if they initially seem daunting. Being open-minded allows you to see change as an opportunity rather than a threat.

3. **Seek Feedback**: Adaptability also means being willing to acknowledge areas for improvement.

There Is No Such Thing as Job Security; There Is Skill Security

Regularly seek feedback from peers, supervisors, or mentors to identify areas where you can grow. This not only helps you improve but also fosters a mindset of continuous development.

4. **Develop Emotional Resilience**: Change can be stressful, but emotional resilience helps you navigate disruptions with grace. Cultivating resilience involves learning how to manage stress, stay positive, and bounce back from setbacks.

A study from the **American Psychological Association (APA)** found that employees with high emotional resilience are better equipped to handle workplace challenges and are more likely to succeed in dynamic environments.

5. **Experiment with New Roles**: Adaptability often involves stepping outside your comfort zone. Volunteer for new projects, take on leadership roles, or explore different aspects of your field. This exposes you to different challenges and builds your capacity to handle various situations.

6. **Expand Your Network**: A diverse professional network exposes you to new ideas, perspectives, and opportunities. Building relationships with individuals from different industries and backgrounds broadens your knowledge and helps you adapt to shifting market trends.

There Is No Such Thing as Job Security; There Is Skill Security

Networking not only helps you stay adaptable, but it also opens doors to new opportunities. According to **Forbes**, 70% of jobs are filled through networking.

How Technology is Shaping Adaptability

The rise of AI, automation, and digital transformation means that technology is driving much of the need for adaptability. According to **Deloitte**, 87% of companies plan to integrate AI into their operations over the next five years. This shift will fundamentally change how we work and what skills are in demand.

While AI may take over certain tasks, it also creates new opportunities for those who can adapt. For instance, while automation can handle repetitive tasks, professionals who excel in areas like **creativity**, **strategic thinking**, and **emotional intelligence** will remain indispensable.

To stay adaptable in this tech-driven landscape, it's essential to:

- **Learn New Technologies**: Continuously upgrade your digital literacy by staying updated on new tools, platforms, and systems relevant to your industry. Whether it's learning a new software program, mastering data analysis, or understanding AI's role in your work, these skills will keep you competitive.

There Is No Such Thing as Job Security; There Is Skill Security

- **Embrace Digital Transformation**: Be open to how technology can enhance your work. For example, using AI tools to streamline processes can free up time for more strategic tasks, allowing you to focus on areas that add greater value.

- **Stay Updated on Industry Trends**: Follow thought leaders, attend webinars, and participate in industry conferences to stay ahead of emerging trends. The faster you adapt to industry changes, the more valuable you will be to employers.

Real-World Examples of Adaptability in Action

Throughout history, adaptability has been a defining trait of successful individuals and companies. Consider the case of **Netflix**, which began as a DVD rental service but successfully adapted to the rise of streaming technology. By embracing change and investing in digital platforms, Netflix transformed itself into a global entertainment powerhouse.

Another example is **IBM**, which shifted from being a hardware company to a leader in cloud computing and AI. By embracing digital transformation, IBM maintained its relevance in the ever-changing tech industry.

On a personal level, professionals who continuously learn and adapt are more likely to advance in their careers. For example, consider the rise of **remote work** during the

There Is No Such Thing as Job Security; There Is Skill Security

COVID-19 pandemic. Those who adapted quickly to digital collaboration tools and remote work processes were able to thrive, while others who struggled with the transition faced difficulties.

According to **McKinsey**, the pandemic accelerated digital adoption by seven years. Professionals who adapted to this shift found themselves well-positioned for new opportunities in a more digital-centric work environment.

The Psychological Benefits of Embracing Adaptability

Beyond the professional advantages, adaptability also provides psychological benefits. When you adopt a flexible mindset, you reduce stress and anxiety related to change. Rather than fearing the unknown, you develop the confidence to handle whatever comes your way.

Research from **Harvard Business School** found that individuals who view change as an opportunity for growth are more likely to experience higher levels of well-being and job satisfaction. This mindset shift helps you stay resilient and positive, even during periods of uncertainty.

Adaptability also fosters a sense of purpose. When you embrace change and continually improve yourself, you build a career that aligns with your passions and values. This sense of purpose increases job satisfaction and helps you navigate challenges with a long-term vision in mind.

There Is No Such Thing as Job Security; There Is Skill Security

Conclusion: Adaptability as a Competitive Advantage

Adaptability is no longer optional—it's a critical skill that ensures long-term success in any industry. The ability to embrace change, learn new technologies, and remain flexible in the face of disruptions will set you apart from your peers.

By cultivating a mindset of continuous learning, staying open to new opportunities, and developing emotional resilience, you can navigate any challenge with confidence. Adaptability not only boosts your self-esteem and self-worth but also positions you as a leader who thrives in dynamic environments.

As industries continue to evolve and technology reshapes the workforce, the most adaptable professionals will be the ones who succeed. Whether you're advancing in your current role or transitioning to a new field, adaptability will ensure that you remain relevant, valuable, and empowered in the face of change. Embrace it, and you'll not only survive but thrive in the modern workplace.

There Is No Such Thing as Job Security; There Is Skill Security

Chapter 7: Networking: Your Lifelong Security Net

In today's fast-paced, competitive world, building a professional network is not just about climbing the corporate ladder; it's about creating a **lifelong security net** that provides opportunities, mentorship, and support at every stage of your career. Networking is the bridge between your personal skills and the opportunities that will help you grow. By establishing strong, meaningful relationships with others, you ensure that you're never alone in navigating the ups and downs of your career. Networking, when done correctly, becomes the foundation for long-term success, helping you thrive even in times of uncertainty.

In this chapter, we will explore how networking impacts self-esteem, self-identity, and career growth. We will dive into the psychological and professional benefits of maintaining a strong network and provide practical tips on how to build and nurture meaningful connections throughout your life.

Why Networking Is Essential in the Modern World

Networking has always been a critical tool for career advancement, but its importance has grown exponentially in recent years. In an age where industries are constantly

There Is No Such Thing as Job Security; There Is Skill Security

evolving, and job roles are shifting rapidly, having a network of professionals who can offer advice, guidance, and opportunities is invaluable. A study by **LinkedIn** found that 85% of all jobs are filled through networking, and another survey by **Harvard Business Review** concluded that 79% of professionals consider networking essential to career success.

While it's often easy to think of networking as just an exchange of business cards or LinkedIn connections, the reality is that it goes much deeper. Effective networking involves building **authentic relationships** based on trust, respect, and mutual value. These relationships can help open doors to new job opportunities, provide mentorship and guidance, and serve as a support system during difficult times.

How Networking Impacts Self-Esteem and Self-Identity

One of the most significant benefits of networking is its positive impact on **self-esteem** and **self-identity**. When you surround yourself with a supportive network of professionals, you gain access to new perspectives, ideas, and resources that reinforce your sense of competence and worth.

Networking helps boost self-esteem by exposing you to people who recognize your skills, talents, and potential. These interactions provide validation, making you feel

There Is No Such Thing as Job Security; There Is Skill Security

more confident in your abilities. A study by the **Journal of Vocational Behavior** found that individuals who maintain strong professional networks report higher levels of self-esteem and job satisfaction, primarily because they feel supported and valued by their peers.

In terms of self-identity, networking plays a crucial role in helping you shape your professional persona. When you engage with others in your industry, you begin to see yourself as part of a larger community of like-minded professionals. This connection to a broader network enhances your sense of belonging and reinforces your professional identity. The more you interact with successful individuals, the more you begin to see yourself as someone capable of achieving great things.

The Power of Weak Ties: Expanding Your Network Beyond Your Inner Circle

One of the most interesting aspects of networking is the importance of **weak ties**—connections you don't interact with regularly but that can provide valuable insights and opportunities. According to sociologist **Mark Granovetter**, weak ties are often more helpful than strong ties when it comes to finding new job opportunities. While your close friends and colleagues might have access to the same information and opportunities as you do, weak ties offer fresh perspectives and access to new networks that you might not otherwise tap into.

There Is No Such Thing as Job Security; There Is Skill Security

Granovetter's research found that 56% of individuals who found new job opportunities did so through weak ties, not close friends. This finding highlights the importance of expanding your network beyond your immediate circle. The more diverse your network, the more likely you are to hear about new opportunities, get introduced to influential people, and stay informed about industry trends.

Building Meaningful Connections: Quality Over Quantity

When it comes to networking, **quality** always trumps quantity. While it might be tempting to focus on collecting as many connections as possible, the real value of networking lies in building **deep, meaningful relationships**. It's better to have a smaller network of people who genuinely know and trust you than to have a large number of superficial contacts.

A study by the **University of California, Berkeley** found that professionals who build deep relationships with their network are more likely to receive career support, mentorship, and opportunities than those who maintain shallow connections. These meaningful relationships are built on trust, reciprocity, and mutual benefit, and they often lead to long-term collaborations and professional growth.

To build meaningful connections, focus on:

There Is No Such Thing as Job Security; There Is Skill Security

1. **Being Authentic**: People are drawn to authenticity. Show genuine interest in others, ask thoughtful questions, and listen actively. Authenticity fosters trust, which is the foundation of any strong relationship.

2. **Offering Value**: Networking is a two-way street. It's important to offer help and value to others, whether it's through sharing resources, offering advice, or connecting people to new opportunities. The more you give, the more you'll receive in return.

3. **Maintaining Regular Contact**: Networking isn't just about meeting someone once—it's about maintaining the relationship over time. Stay in touch with your contacts, offer updates on your career, and check in with them regularly.

4. **Following Up**: After meeting someone new, always follow up with a thoughtful message or email. Reiterate your appreciation for the connection and express your interest in keeping in touch. This simple gesture can make a significant difference in building long-lasting relationships.

Mentorship: The Lifelong Value of a Strong Mentor

One of the greatest benefits of networking is the opportunity to find **mentorship**. A mentor can provide

There Is No Such Thing as Job Security; There Is Skill Security

guidance, support, and wisdom that accelerates your personal and professional growth. According to a **Harvard Business Review** survey, 71% of professionals with mentors said that their mentor directly contributed to their career success.

Finding a mentor through networking can be transformative. A mentor offers more than just career advice—they provide a **sounding board** for your ideas, help you navigate challenges, and share insights from their own experiences. A mentor can also introduce you to valuable contacts, recommend you for new opportunities, and offer feedback on your career decisions.

To find a mentor, consider reaching out to someone in your industry whom you admire. Look for individuals who share your values and have a track record of success in areas you'd like to grow. When approaching a potential mentor, be respectful of their time and express your desire to learn from them. Many professionals are eager to give back by mentoring the next generation of leaders.

Leveraging Social Media for Networking

In today's digital age, **social media platforms** like LinkedIn, Twitter, and even Instagram have become invaluable tools for networking. These platforms allow you to connect with professionals around the world, share your expertise, and stay updated on industry trends. According

There Is No Such Thing as Job Security; There Is Skill Security

to a **Jobvite** survey, 87% of recruiters use LinkedIn to vet candidates, underscoring the importance of maintaining a strong online presence.

To effectively leverage social media for networking:

- **Optimize Your LinkedIn Profile**: Your LinkedIn profile is often the first impression you make on potential employers and colleagues. Ensure that it's up-to-date, showcases your skills and accomplishments, and includes a professional photo. Post regularly about industry trends, articles, and your own achievements to engage your network.

- **Engage with Others**: Networking on social media isn't just about posting your content—it's about engaging with others. Comment on posts, share insights, and congratulate people on their accomplishments. This engagement helps you build relationships and stay top-of-mind in your network.

- **Join Industry Groups**: Many social media platforms have groups or communities where professionals gather to discuss industry-specific topics. Joining these groups allows you to meet new people, learn from others, and expand your network beyond your immediate connections.

There Is No Such Thing as Job Security; There Is Skill Security

The Long-Term Benefits of Networking: Career Growth and Job Security

Networking provides a **lifelong security net** that offers opportunities, mentorship, and support throughout your career. While job security can fluctuate, having a strong network ensures that you always have access to new opportunities, advice, and connections. In fact, **Forbes** reports that 70% of people secure jobs through their network rather than through traditional job postings.

One of the long-term benefits of networking is the ability to **navigate career transitions** more smoothly. Whether you're switching industries, seeking a promotion, or facing a layoff, your network can provide invaluable guidance and referrals that help you stay on track.

Networking also offers opportunities for **career growth**. Professionals who maintain strong networks are more likely to be recommended for promotions, invited to join leadership teams, and offered new projects. A **Harvard Business Review** study found that individuals with strong networks are 42% more likely to achieve their career goals than those with weak or nonexistent networks.

Conclusion: Networking as a Lifelong Investment

Networking is more than just a career strategy—it's a lifelong investment in your personal and professional growth. By building and maintaining a strong network, you

There Is No Such Thing as Job Security; There Is Skill Security

create a support system that will help you navigate career challenges, seize new opportunities, and find mentorship along the way. Networking boosts your self-esteem, enhances your self-identity, and provides the security of knowing that you're never alone in your career journey.

As you move forward in your professional life, remember that networking is not just about what others can do for you—it's about building authentic, meaningful relationships that benefit everyone involved. The stronger your network, the more resilient and adaptable you become, ensuring that you can thrive in any environment. So, take the time to invest in your relationships, offer value to others, and stay open to the endless opportunities that networking provides.

There Is No Such Thing as Job Security; There Is Skill Security

Chapter 8: Side Projects and Freelancing for Security

In a world where traditional job security is becoming increasingly uncertain, developing **side projects** and engaging in **freelance work** can be powerful strategies for diversifying income streams and ensuring financial security. Side projects are not just about making extra money—they provide an opportunity to pursue your passions, enhance your skills, and explore new industries or markets. For many, side hustles evolve into full-time careers, offering greater flexibility and control over their professional lives.

This chapter will explore how side projects and freelancing can boost your **self-esteem**, **self-identity**, and **career growth**, offering practical steps for getting started, staying motivated, and managing your time effectively. We'll examine studies that highlight the benefits of freelancing and explore real-world examples of individuals who have successfully turned their side projects into thriving careers.

The Rise of the Gig Economy: A New Era of Work

The rise of the **gig economy**—a labor market characterized by freelance work, short-term contracts, and independent gigs—has fundamentally reshaped the world of work. Today, millions of people around the globe are

There Is No Such Thing as Job Security; There Is Skill Security

participating in the gig economy, leveraging their skills and passions to create multiple streams of income. A 2020 study by **Upwork** revealed that **36% of the U.S. workforce** is engaged in freelancing, contributing over $1.2 trillion to the economy annually.

The growth of the gig economy has been fueled by technological advancements, such as online platforms that connect freelancers with clients, and the increasing demand for flexible work arrangements. Whether you're an artist, writer, software developer, marketer, or consultant, there are countless opportunities to monetize your skills and interests through side projects or freelancing.

One of the key benefits of the gig economy is the **diversification of income**. Relying on a single job or employer can be risky in today's volatile job market, but having multiple streams of income provides a safety net. If one stream dries up, others can keep you afloat, offering greater financial security and peace of mind.

How Side Projects and Freelancing Boost Self-Esteem and Self-Worth

Engaging in side projects or freelancing offers significant psychological benefits, particularly in terms of **self-esteem** and **self-worth**. When you work on projects that align with your passions or allow you to showcase your talents, you gain a sense of accomplishment and pride in your abilities.

There Is No Such Thing as Job Security; There Is Skill Security

Each new project completed or freelance contract secured reinforces your belief in your capabilities, boosting your confidence and self-esteem.

Freelancing also allows you to take ownership of your work. Unlike traditional employment, where you may be confined to a specific role or set of tasks, freelancing gives you the freedom to choose the projects you work on and the clients you collaborate with. This autonomy fosters a sense of **self-empowerment**, as you are in control of your professional journey.

A study by the **Freelancers Union** found that **72% of freelancers** report feeling more fulfilled and satisfied with their work compared to traditional employees. This sense of fulfillment comes from the ability to work on projects that are meaningful and aligned with personal goals, rather than simply fulfilling the requirements of an employer.

Side Projects as a Path to Skill Development

One of the most compelling reasons to start a side project is the opportunity it provides for **skill development**. Side projects allow you to experiment, learn, and grow in ways that might not be possible in your primary job. Whether you're learning a new programming language, refining your design skills, or exploring a creative hobby, side projects are an excellent way to **enhance your skill set** and stay competitive in the job market.

There Is No Such Thing as Job Security; There Is Skill Security

In fact, many employers value candidates who demonstrate initiative through side projects. According to a study by **LinkedIn**, 92% of hiring managers are more likely to hire someone with a side project or freelance experience, as it shows that the individual is proactive, self-motivated, and continuously learning.

Side projects can also serve as a way to **transition into a new career**. For example, if you're interested in switching from marketing to web development, starting a freelance web development business on the side can help you build the necessary skills and portfolio to make that transition. This gradual shift allows you to gain experience and confidence without the financial risk of quitting your full-time job.

Freelancing for Financial Security

Freelancing not only offers opportunities for personal growth but also provides **financial security** in an increasingly unpredictable job market. By developing multiple income streams, you reduce your dependence on a single employer and create a buffer against job loss, economic downturns, or unexpected life events.

According to a 2019 study by **McKinsey**, 60% of freelancers reported that they chose freelancing to gain more control over their income, while 46% cited increased flexibility as a key motivator. Freelancers have the ability

There Is No Such Thing as Job Security; There Is Skill Security

to set their own rates, take on as many or as few clients as they wish, and choose the projects that best align with their financial goals.

Freelancing can also be particularly valuable for individuals who work in industries that are prone to layoffs or job instability. For example, during the COVID-19 pandemic, many full-time employees faced furloughs or layoffs, while freelancers were able to continue working remotely and securing new contracts through online platforms. This flexibility and adaptability make freelancing a valuable tool for long-term financial resilience.

Finding Your Passion Project: What Should You Pursue?

One of the most exciting aspects of starting a side project or freelance business is the ability to pursue work that genuinely excites you. The key to finding the right passion project is to identify an area where your interests, skills, and market demand intersect.

Here are a few steps to help you discover the right side project or freelance gig for you:

1. **Identify Your Skills and Interests**: Start by making a list of your skills, hobbies, and areas of expertise. What are you passionate about? What do you enjoy doing in your free time? These interests

There Is No Such Thing as Job Security; There Is Skill Security

can often serve as the foundation for a side project or freelance gig.

2. **Research Market Demand**: Once you've identified your interests, research the market demand for those skills. Are there opportunities to monetize your talents? For example, if you're a graphic designer, you might explore freelance design work, creating digital products, or offering design courses online.

3. **Start Small**: You don't need to launch a full-fledged business overnight. Start with a small project or freelance gig that allows you to test the waters. This could be a weekend side hustle, a short-term freelance contract, or a creative project that you work on in your spare time.

4. **Leverage Online Platforms**: There are countless online platforms that connect freelancers with clients, such as **Upwork**, **Fiverr**, **Freelancer**, and **Toptal**. These platforms offer opportunities for professionals across a wide range of industries, from writing and design to programming and consulting. By creating a profile and showcasing your work, you can attract clients and start building your freelance portfolio.

There Is No Such Thing as Job Security; There Is Skill Security

5. **Set Clear Goals**: Establish clear goals for your side project or freelance work. Are you looking to generate extra income, develop new skills, or eventually transition into a full-time freelance career? Having a clear sense of purpose will help you stay focused and motivated.

Managing Time and Avoiding Burnout

While side projects and freelancing offer numerous benefits, it's essential to manage your time effectively to avoid **burnout**. Juggling a full-time job, personal responsibilities, and a side hustle can be challenging, but with the right strategies, it's possible to maintain balance and prevent exhaustion.

Here are some practical tips for managing your time while pursuing side projects:

1. **Set Boundaries**: Establish clear boundaries between your full-time job and your side project. Dedicate specific hours each week to your side hustle, and make sure that it doesn't interfere with your primary job or personal life.

2. **Prioritize Tasks**: Identify the most important tasks for both your full-time job and your side project. Focus on high-impact activities that will move the needle forward in your side hustle, rather than getting caught up in low-priority tasks.

There Is No Such Thing as Job Security; There Is Skill Security

3. **Use Time-Blocking**: Time-blocking is a powerful technique for managing your time and staying focused. Schedule dedicated blocks of time for different activities, such as client work, skill development, and personal projects. This helps you stay organized and ensures that you're making progress on both your side hustle and your full-time job.

4. **Delegate When Possible**: If your side project begins to grow, consider outsourcing or delegating tasks to others. Hiring freelancers or contractors to handle administrative tasks, marketing, or design work can free up your time to focus on the core aspects of your business.

5. **Take Breaks**: Finally, don't forget to take breaks and recharge. Side projects and freelancing can be incredibly rewarding, but they can also lead to burnout if you're constantly working without rest. Make time for relaxation, hobbies, and self-care to maintain your energy and motivation.

Turning Your Side Hustle Into a Full-Time Career

For many professionals, side projects and freelance work start as a way to supplement income or explore a passion, but they eventually evolve into full-time careers. According to **MBO Partners**, more than **41 million Americans** are

There Is No Such Thing as Job Security; There Is Skill Security

now working as independent professionals, and that number is expected to grow as more people seek the freedom and flexibility of self-employment.

If you're considering turning your side hustle into a full-time career, here are a few steps to help you make the transition:

1. **Build a Client Base**: Before quitting your full-time job, focus on building a solid client base for your freelance business. This provides a steady stream of income and reduces the financial risk of transitioning to full-time freelancing.

2. **Develop a Financial PlanFreelancing and side projects have become viable strategies for enhancing both personal and professional security in an unpredictable world. By developing side hustles, you not only diversify your income streams but also create opportunities to pursue passions, develop new skills, and position yourself for career growth. Studies, such as those from **Upwork** and **McKinsey**, show that freelancing provides financial security, skill enhancement, and even personal fulfillment for many professionals.

This chapter explores how side projects and freelance work boost **self-esteem**, **self-worth**, and provide a sense of

There Is No Such Thing as Job Security; There Is Skill Security

control over one's career, alongside practical steps for getting started and scaling.

The Power of Side Projects and Freelancing

Engaging in side projects enables you to take ownership of your work and build something outside the structure of your full-time job. Whether you're designing websites, writing content, creating apps, or offering consultancy services, these activities foster **self-reliance** and boost **confidence**. For example, if you're an engineer by day but passionate about photography, freelancing in photography can be a way to turn that passion into profit. In doing so, you gain new clients, build your reputation, and enhance your financial security, all while pursuing something you genuinely enjoy.

According to the **Freelancers Union, 57 million** Americans freelanced in 2021, and that number is growing. The report also shows that 75% of freelancers consider it a long-term career choice because it offers autonomy and flexibility that traditional jobs may not. Side projects allow you to pursue work on your terms and build a **personal brand** that distinguishes you in the marketplace.

Enhancing Skills and Staying Competitive

The ability to **learn and apply new skills** is one of the greatest benefits of freelancing and side projects. These ventures expose you to new tools, platforms, and

There Is No Such Thing as Job Security; There Is Skill Security

challenges that help you grow in ways a single, stable job often can't. For instance, if you're in a tech job, a side project could involve experimenting with new coding languages, allowing you to stay ahead of industry trends. For those in creative fields, freelancing in writing, design, or marketing can help develop a more diverse portfolio that appeals to a broad range of clients.

A study by **McKinsey** revealed that **up to 87% of executives** report gaps in key digital skills in their organizations. Freelancers who develop a niche expertise in areas like digital marketing, data science, or app development are in high demand. Side projects enable you to fill these gaps and position yourself as a **go-to expert** in those fields.

Building Financial Resilience

Financial independence is a significant motivator for many freelancers and side hustlers. Having multiple income streams from side projects or freelance work reduces your reliance on a single employer, which provides greater financial security. In case of a job loss, economic downturn, or personal emergency, you'll have another source of income to fall back on.

A report from **Statista** showed that **70% of freelancers** do so to supplement their income, while 43% said freelancing helped them save for unexpected financial challenges. This

There Is No Such Thing as Job Security; There Is Skill Security

highlights the importance of freelancing as a strategy for **building financial resilience**. Whether your goal is to pay off debt, save for retirement, or fund a passion project, side work can accelerate your financial goals while giving you more control over your earnings.

Choosing the Right Side Project

Not every side hustle or freelance project is worth pursuing. To choose the right side project, consider aligning your skills, passions, and market demand. Here's how to narrow it down:

1. **Identify Your Skills and Strengths**: What are you good at? Are there any skills from your day job that you can monetize? Perhaps you're a talented writer or a great graphic designer. Recognizing your strengths is the first step in finding a profitable side hustle.

2. **Align with Your Interests**: Pursue something you're passionate about. If you're passionate about technology, start a tech blog. If you love design, explore freelance web design. Passion keeps you motivated, especially when managing a full-time job and a side hustle.

3. **Research Market Demand**: You may love something, but does it align with what people are willing to pay for? Use platforms like **Upwork**,

There Is No Such Thing as Job Security; There Is Skill Security

    Fiverr, or **Freelancer** to gauge demand for certain services. Look for gaps in the market where your skill set can provide value.

4. **Start Small and Scale**: It's best to start with small, manageable projects that fit into your schedule. As you gain experience, you can gradually take on more clients, increase your rates, or expand into other areas.

Practical Steps for Freelancing Success

If you're ready to take the leap into freelancing or launching a side project, here are a few practical steps to help you succeed:

1. **Build a Portfolio**: Whether you're starting in design, marketing, writing, or coding, having a portfolio that showcases your best work is crucial. Use platforms like **Behance** for designers, **GitHub** for developers, or create your own website using platforms like **WordPress**.

2. **Join Freelance Platforms**: Freelance platforms like **Upwork, Fiverr, PeoplePerHour**, and **Freelancer** offer access to clients looking for specific services. These platforms allow you to bid for projects, get client reviews, and build a reputation.

There Is No Such Thing as Job Security; There Is Skill Security

3. **Set Realistic Goals**: Freelancing can be a slow start, so set manageable goals. Start with part-time freelancing and aim to secure one or two small clients a month. Over time, as your network grows, you can scale up.

4. **Time Management**: Balancing a full-time job and a side project requires excellent time management. Use tools like **Trello** or **Asana** to keep track of deadlines, manage tasks, and ensure you're meeting both client and employer expectations.

5. **Stay Organized**: Managing finances, clients, and personal projects can get overwhelming. Make sure you keep your income streams organized, track invoices, and set aside money for taxes if you're working as an independent contractor.

Freelancing to Full-Time Freedom

Many successful freelancers started with side projects before transitioning into full-time careers. For those looking to make freelancing their primary source of income, the journey often begins with balancing both worlds. According to a study by **MBO Partners**, **42 million people** in the U.S. work as full-time independent professionals, and more are making this transition as they find success in their freelancing endeavors.

There Is No Such Thing as Job Security; There Is Skill Security

The key to transitioning is knowing when your freelance income becomes stable enough to support you full-time. Some signs that you're ready to transition include:

- **Consistent Client Base**: You have regular clients who provide a steady stream of work.

- **Financial Stability**: Your freelance income matches or exceeds your full-time salary, and you have enough saved to cover potential slow periods.

- **Professional Reputation**: You've built a solid reputation in your industry, with testimonials and referrals coming in regularly.

By planning your transition carefully, you can turn your side hustle into a sustainable, long-term career that offers flexibility, financial freedom, and personal fulfillment.

The Future of Work: Freelancing as a Security Net

As the gig economy continues to grow, freelancing will increasingly become a part of the future workforce. The **World Economic Forum** predicts that by 2030, **50% of the U.S. workforce** will be engaged in freelance work. This shift underscores the importance of building **self-reliance** and maintaining multiple income streams.

Freelancing is not just about diversifying your income—it's about creating a **lifelong security net** that offers flexibility, control, and fulfillment. The ability to adapt, develop new

There Is No Such Thing as Job Security; There Is Skill Security

skills, and pursue your passions outside of traditional employment ensures that you remain **financially resilient** and professionally relevant, no matter how the job market evolves.

Conclusion: Side Projects and Freelancing for Security

Side projects and freelancing are powerful tools for building **financial security**, enhancing your **skills**, and providing long-term career flexibility. They offer a unique combination of personal fulfillment, professional growth, and economic resilience that traditional employment alone cannot provide.

By pursuing side hustles that align with your passions and skills, you can diversify your income streams, protect yourself against economic uncertainty, and develop a reputation as a skilled professional in your field. Whether your goal is to supplement your income or transition into full-time freelancing, the benefits of starting a side project are immense.

In today's ever-changing job market, side projects and freelancing aren't just a trend—they're a necessity for ensuring long-term career success. By taking control of your professional journey, you can build a career that offers both **financial freedom** and personal fulfillment.

There Is No Such Thing as Job Security; There Is Skill Security

Chapter 9: Upskill for the Future: Continuous Learning Plans

In today's fast-evolving world, marked by rapid technological advancement and industry disruptions, continuous learning has become essential for both personal and professional growth. Upskilling is no longer just about improving career prospects but is a critical component for maintaining relevance in a dynamic marketplace. This chapter delves into the importance of upskilling, how to develop a continuous learning habit, and offers practical steps to future-proof your career.

Upskilling is a proactive approach to adapting to industry changes, improving self-esteem, and boosting self-worth. It's about staying ahead of the curve and building the skills necessary to thrive in an environment where technologies like artificial intelligence (AI), automation, and digitalization are reshaping industries.

Why Upskilling Is Vital for the Future

With the rapid pace of technological advancement, job roles are evolving, and entire industries are being redefined. According to the **World Economic Forum**, by 2025, **50% of all employees** will need reskilling due to automation and other technological innovations. Many traditional roles are

There Is No Such Thing as Job Security; There Is Skill Security

being phased out, while new positions are emerging that require specialized skills, particularly in data science, AI, digital marketing, and cybersecurity.

In the context of these changes, continuous learning is the best way to ensure you remain adaptable and capable of meeting the demands of the future workplace. Upskilling not only keeps you competitive in your current role but also equips you to transition into new industries or take on more advanced responsibilities.

A report by **McKinsey & Company** found that **87% of executives** are either experiencing skills gaps in their workforce or expect them within the next few years. As a result, companies are increasingly prioritizing employees who demonstrate a commitment to lifelong learning. For individuals, this means that the ability to learn and adapt is now just as critical as job performance.

The Psychological Benefits of Continuous Learning

Upskilling provides profound psychological benefits that extend beyond professional growth. Engaging in continuous learning fosters a **growth mindset**, a concept developed by psychologist **Carol Dweck**. A growth mindset is the belief that abilities and intelligence can be developed through dedication and hard work. This mindset fosters resilience and motivation, encouraging individuals

There Is No Such Thing as Job Security; There Is Skill Security

to embrace challenges and see failures as opportunities for growth.

As you acquire new skills, you build confidence in your ability to tackle new challenges, leading to enhanced **self-esteem**. Every course completed, certification earned, or new skill mastered reinforces the belief that you are capable of growth and improvement. This sense of accomplishment extends beyond the workplace and contributes to an overall sense of well-being.

Furthermore, continuous learning helps shape your **self-identity** as a professional who is committed to development and innovation. When you view yourself as someone who is always evolving, you are more likely to seek out new challenges, take on leadership roles, and seize opportunities that others may shy away from.

Building a Continuous Learning Plan: Practical Steps

1. **Identify Industry Trends and Future Skills**

The first step in upskilling is understanding the **trends** that are shaping your industry. New technologies, regulatory changes, and shifting consumer behaviors often lead to demand for new skills. For instance, industries like healthcare, finance, and manufacturing are increasingly reliant on data analytics, AI, and automation. Therefore, upskilling in areas like machine learning, cloud computing, and data science is becoming more important.

There Is No Such Thing as Job Security; There Is Skill Security

Stay informed about industry developments by following trade publications, joining professional organizations, and attending conferences. Use online resources such as **Google Trends, LinkedIn Learning,** or **Harvard Business Review** to stay up to date on emerging trends. By doing so, you can identify the skills that will be in demand and plan your learning accordingly.

2. Assess Your Current Skills and Knowledge Gaps

Conduct a **self-assessment** to evaluate your current skill set and identify areas for improvement. This involves reviewing your technical and soft skills and determining where gaps exist. Consider seeking feedback from supervisors, peers, or mentors to gain a more comprehensive understanding of your strengths and areas for development.

Use tools like **SkillsGap Analysis** or career development frameworks to systematically identify the skills you need to advance. For example, if you're a marketer, you might find that digital marketing and SEO are critical areas for growth. If you're in IT, cloud computing or cybersecurity may be areas where you need to focus your efforts.

3. Set Clear, Achievable Learning Goals

Once you've identified the skills you need, set **SMART goals**—Specific, Measurable, Achievable, Relevant, and Time-bound—to guide your learning journey. For example,

There Is No Such Thing as Job Security; There Is Skill Security

rather than setting a vague goal like "improve my coding skills," aim for something concrete, such as "complete an advanced Python programming course within three months."

By breaking your goals down into smaller, manageable steps, you make the learning process less overwhelming and more achievable. These smaller milestones also help to maintain motivation as you experience steady progress.

4. **Leverage Online Learning Platforms**

With the proliferation of **e-learning platforms**, upskilling has never been more accessible. Platforms such as **Coursera, edX, Udemy,** and **LinkedIn Learning** offer a wide range of courses in everything from software development and data science to leadership and communication skills. Many courses provide certifications, which are highly valued by employers.

Online learning allows you to learn at your own pace, making it easier to balance continuous learning with full-time work. In fact, a survey by **LinkedIn Learning** found that professionals who dedicate time to learning are **30% more likely to be promoted** than those who don't.

5. **Earn Certifications for Credibility**

In addition to taking courses, earning industry-recognized **certifications** is an excellent way to demonstrate your

There Is No Such Thing as Job Security; There Is Skill Security

expertise to potential employers. Certifications validate your skills and show that you are committed to continuous professional development. Examples include certifications in **Google Analytics**, **AWS Certified Solutions Architect**, and **PMP (Project Management Professional)**.

According to **Statista**, professionals with certifications in relevant fields, such as project management or data science, earn on average **13% more** than their uncertified counterparts. These credentials can set you apart in a competitive job market and open doors to higher-paying roles.

6. Incorporate Learning into Your Daily Routine

One of the most effective ways to maintain a habit of continuous learning is to make it part of your **daily routine**. Set aside a specific time each day for learning, whether that's reading an industry article during your lunch break, watching a webinar in the evening, or taking an online course over the weekend. Consistent learning, even in small doses, leads to long-term growth.

Use productivity tools like **Notion**, **Trello**, or **Google Calendar** to schedule your learning activities and keep track of your progress. These tools allow you to break down your learning goals into smaller tasks, making the process more manageable and keeping you accountable.

7. Apply What You Learn

There Is No Such Thing as Job Security; There Is Skill Security

Learning without application leads to limited growth. To truly master new skills, you must **apply them** in real-world scenarios. Whether it's taking on new responsibilities at work, volunteering for a leadership role, or working on side projects, hands-on experience is the best way to solidify your knowledge.

A **Harvard Business Review** study emphasizes that experiential learning—learning by doing—is one of the most effective methods for acquiring new skills. Applying your knowledge not only reinforces what you've learned but also gives you tangible experience to showcase to future employers.

8. **Seek Mentorship and Feedback**

Mentorship plays a crucial role in your learning journey. Mentors can provide guidance, feedback, and insight into the skills and competencies needed to succeed in your industry. According to research by **Gallup**, employees who have mentors are five times more likely to be promoted than those who do not.

Engaging with mentors and professional networks accelerates learning and exposes you to opportunities that might not be accessible through formal training programs. Mentors can also help you stay motivated and offer encouragement when faced with challenges.

The Role of AI and Automation in Upskilling

There Is No Such Thing as Job Security; There Is Skill Security

The rise of **AI and automation** has fundamentally changed the skills landscape. While automation may eliminate certain routine jobs, it also creates new opportunities for those with advanced technical and digital skills. A report by **PwC** predicts that AI will create **133 million new jobs** by 2025, particularly in fields like **data science**, **robotics engineering**, and **AI ethics**.

Professionals who upskill in these areas will not only remain competitive but will also position themselves as leaders in emerging fields. AI will drive demand for roles that require creative problem-solving, data analysis, and human-centered skills—areas where automation cannot fully replace human input.

Upskilling for Career Resilience

Continuous learning fosters **career resilience**, the ability to adapt to industry changes and bounce back from setbacks. A study by **Deloitte** found that professionals who engage in upskilling report higher levels of job satisfaction and are more likely to remain engaged in their work.

In a rapidly changing job market, career resilience is essential. Whether it's developing new technical skills or enhancing soft skills like leadership and communication, upskilling equips you to navigate industry shifts and take advantage of new opportunities.

Real-World Examples of Upskilling Success

There Is No Such Thing as Job Security; There Is Skill Security

Countless professionals have successfully transitioned into new roles through upskilling. For instance, individuals in marketing or finance have taken online courses in **data science** and **AI**, allowing them to transition into higher-paying roles within the tech industry. Platforms like **Kaggle** and **DataCamp** provide hands-on learning opportunities for those looking to master data analytics and machine learning.

Similarly, **project managers** who have earned certifications in **Agile** or **Scrum** methodologies are well-positioned to lead teams in organizations adopting these practices. These examples### Chapter 9: **Upskill for the Future: Continuous Learning Plans**

In the modern workforce, continuous learning is vital to maintaining relevance and thriving amidst rapid technological change. Upskilling is no longer optional—it's essential for both personal development and career resilience. This chapter explores the benefits of lifelong learning, provides a practical roadmap for identifying industry trends, and outlines how to stay competitive through courses, certifications, and proactive self-development.

Why Upskilling Is Critical in Today's Workforce

The accelerating pace of technological innovation has created a workplace where skills that were once in demand

There Is No Such Thing as Job Security; There Is Skill Security

can quickly become obsolete. Roles that depend on automation or outdated technologies are particularly vulnerable. **According to the World Economic Forum, 50% of all employees** will need reskilling by 2025 due to the rise of AI and automation. These technologies are transforming every sector, from healthcare to finance, and professionals who fail to adapt risk being left behind.

This shift highlights the importance of **upskilling**—the process of learning new skills or improving existing ones to stay relevant. For example, industries such as **data analytics, AI, cybersecurity**, and **digital marketing** are witnessing increased demand for skilled professionals. Those who continually invest in learning are better positioned to adapt to market changes and seize emerging opportunities.

Additionally, a **McKinsey & Company** report showed that **87% of executives** already see skills gaps in their workforce or anticipate such gaps in the near future. This indicates that companies are looking for employees who are committed to continuous learning and development.

The Psychological Benefits of Continuous Learning

Upskilling provides not only professional but also significant **psychological benefits**. When you engage in continuous learning, you reinforce a **growth mindset**—the belief that abilities and intelligence can be developed

There Is No Such Thing as Job Security; There Is Skill Security

through effort, learning, and persistence. This mindset, popularized by psychologist **Carol Dweck**, helps individuals embrace challenges, view failure as a stepping stone, and remain resilient.

Moreover, learning new skills boosts **self-esteem**. Each course completed or certification earned reinforces your belief in your abilities. As you grow more confident in your skillset, you naturally take on more challenging projects and responsibilities, which further enhances your sense of competence and self-worth.

Upskilling also enhances **self-identity**. When you see yourself as someone who is constantly evolving, learning, and adapting, it influences how you approach challenges and opportunities. You begin to view yourself as a proactive individual who thrives in dynamic environments, which opens doors to leadership roles and greater career opportunities.

Building a Continuous Learning Plan: Practical Steps

To effectively upskill, it's crucial to create a well-defined learning plan. Below are key steps for building an actionable and successful upskilling roadmap:

1. Identify Industry Trends and In-Demand Skills

The first step in any learning plan is to understand the **trends** shaping your industry. Technology is driving rapid

There Is No Such Thing as Job Security; There Is Skill Security

changes, and new skills are constantly emerging. For instance, areas such as **AI**, **machine learning**, and **blockchain** are becoming more integral to fields like finance, healthcare, and retail.

To stay ahead, regularly review industry reports, attend conferences, and follow thought leaders on platforms like **LinkedIn**. Publications such as **Harvard Business Review** and **Deloitte** often release reports that highlight the emerging skills most in demand. By staying informed, you can anticipate the skills your industry will need in the coming years and adjust your learning plan accordingly.

2. **Assess Your Current Skills and Knowledge Gaps**

Conduct a thorough **skills audit** to evaluate your current strengths and identify gaps in your knowledge. What skills do you already possess? What areas need improvement? For example, if you're working in marketing, you might need to sharpen your digital advertising skills or familiarize yourself with data analytics tools like **Google Analytics**.

Use self-assessment tools such as **StrengthsFinder** or take feedback from colleagues and supervisors to identify areas where you need development. This assessment will help you focus your upskilling efforts on the most critical areas for growth.

3. **Set SMART Learning Goals**

There Is No Such Thing as Job Security; There Is Skill Security

Setting clear, actionable goals is essential for any successful learning plan. Use the **SMART framework**—Specific, Measurable, Achievable, Relevant, and Time-bound—when setting your goals. For example, instead of saying, "I want to learn data science," set a more specific goal: "I will complete a certification in **Python programming** in six months."

Break your learning objectives down into smaller, manageable milestones. This will make the process feel less overwhelming and help you stay motivated as you progress. Regularly reviewing and adjusting these goals ensures that your learning stays aligned with your overall career aspirations.

4. Leverage Online Learning Platforms

In today's digital age, a wealth of learning resources is available at your fingertips. Platforms like **Coursera**, **edX**, **Udemy**, and **LinkedIn Learning** offer courses in everything from AI and data science to leadership and emotional intelligence. Many courses provide certifications that you can add to your resume or **LinkedIn** profile, signaling your skills to employers.

According to a survey by **LinkedIn Learning**, professionals who engage in continuous learning are **30% more likely to be promoted** than their peers who don't. Online learning is flexible, allowing you to learn at your

There Is No Such Thing as Job Security; There Is Skill Security

own pace and on your own schedule, making it easier to balance work and personal life.

5. **Earn Certifications for Credibility**

Certifications add credibility to your skills, especially in technical fields. Industry-recognized certifications, such as **Google Cloud Certifications**, **AWS Certified Solutions Architect**, or **PMP (Project Management Professional)**, are highly valuable. These certifications serve as proof of your expertise and are often required for advanced roles.

A **Statista** report shows that professionals with certifications can earn **13% more** than those without them. Obtaining these credentials not only boosts your earning potential but also makes you more competitive in the job market.

6. **Incorporate Learning into Your Daily Routine**

To ensure you make steady progress, integrate learning into your **daily routine**. Set aside time each day or week for learning activities, such as reading industry-related articles, watching tutorials, or completing course modules. Consistent, small efforts lead to significant improvements over time.

Tools like **Google Calendar**, **Notion**, and **Trello** can help you stay organized and on track. By scheduling learning

There Is No Such Thing as Job Security; There Is Skill Security

sessions and breaking down larger goals into smaller tasks, you make it easier to maintain your momentum.

7. Apply What You Learn in Real-World Scenarios

Learning becomes more valuable when you apply it in real-world contexts. Whether it's taking on new responsibilities at work, volunteering for challenging projects, or working on **side projects**, hands-on experience allows you to test and refine your skills.

A **Harvard Business Review** study emphasizes the importance of **experiential learning**—learning by doing—as one of the most effective ways to master new skills. This approach not only enhances your understanding but also provides tangible proof of your abilities for future employers.

8. Seek Feedback and Mentorship

Mentorship is an invaluable tool for upskilling. A mentor can provide guidance, help you navigate challenges, and offer insights based on their experience. Studies by **Gallup** show that employees with mentors are **five times more likely** to be promoted than those without.

Additionally, seeking feedback from peers or supervisors helps you assess your progress and identify areas for improvement. Continuous feedback ensures that your

There Is No Such Thing as Job Security; There Is Skill Security

learning is aligned with industry standards and expectations.

The Role of AI and Automation in Upskilling

The integration of **AI and automation** into various industries has transformed the job market. While these technologies may displace certain roles, they also create opportunities for professionals with the right skills. According to **PwC**, AI will create **133 million new jobs** by 2025, particularly in areas such as data analysis, AI development, and robotics engineering.

Professionals who upskill in these areas will be well-positioned to capitalize on the demand for expertise in AI, automation, and other emerging fields. The rise of AI also means that roles requiring **creative problem-solving**, **emotional intelligence**, and **strategic thinking** will be in high demand, as these are areas where humans have a distinct advantage over machines.

Real-World Examples of Upskilling Success

Consider the example of **data science**, which has seen a surge in demand across industries. Many professionals with backgrounds in marketing, finance, or operations have successfully transitioned into data science roles by completing online courses and earning certifications in **Python, R programming**, and **machine learning**. Platforms like **Kaggle** and **DataCamp** offer hands-on

There Is No Such Thing as Job Security; There Is Skill Security

earning opportunities for those looking to break into this field.

Similarly, professionals in project management who earned certifications in **Agile** or **Scrum** methodologies have found themselves leading teams in organizations that are adopting these frameworks. These certifications have not only improved their technical capabilities but also positioned them for leadership roles in a rapidly evolving job market.

The Future of Work: Lifelong Learning Is Essential

As technology continues to evolve, the future of work will require professionals who are agile, adaptable, and committed to continuous learning. A **Deloitte** study found that employees who embrace lifelong learning report higher levels of **job satisfaction** and are more likely to remain engaged in their careers.

The key to staying competitive in this future landscape is **career resilience**—the ability to adapt to change, overcome setbacks, and continue growing professionally. Whether it's through online learning, mentorship, or hands-on experience, upskilling ensures that you remain at the forefront of industry developments and well-positioned to take on new challenges.

Conclusion

There Is No Such Thing as Job Security; There Is Skill Security

In conclusion, upskilling is essential for future-proofing your career in a rapidly changing world. By developing a habit of continuous learning, you can adapt to industry trends, improve your self-esteem, and boost your professional value. Whether through online courses, certifications, or mentorship, consistent learning empowers you to stay relevant, build resilience, and thrive in a dynamic job market. As AI and automation reshape industries, those who invest in their skills will remain competitive and well-positioned for future opportunities. Continuous learning is your most valuable asset.

**There Is No Such Thing as Job Security;
There Is Skill Security**

Chapter 10: Own Your Career Growth: Measure, Track, and Improve

Taking ownership of your career growth is not just an option—it's essential for staying competitive in today's ever-evolving workplace. This chapter will inspire and guide you to take control of your professional development by setting goals, measuring your impact, and tracking both your hard and soft skills. By cultivating a proactive approach to your career progression, you can improve your self-esteem, build your skills, and ultimately position yourself for long-term success.

The Importance of Taking Ownership of Your Career Growth

In the rapidly changing modern workplace, career growth is not something that can be left to chance or depend solely on an employer. With advancements in technology and the rising complexity of industries, professionals must take an active role in defining, measuring, and improving their career trajectory. A **Gallup report** found that 70% of employees feel disengaged at work, often because they don't feel in control of their professional development. When you take ownership of your career growth, you

There Is No Such Thing as Job Security; There Is Skill Security

become empowered to define your success and create opportunities that align with your ambitions.

Owning your career growth doesn't mean just aiming for promotions or salary increases. It involves **self-improvement** in various areas such as **soft skills**, **hard skills**, leadership capabilities, and emotional intelligence. Moreover, career ownership boosts **self-esteem** and **self-worth** by affirming that your progress is not dictated by external factors but by your personal efforts.

Setting Clear, Actionable Career Goals

The first step in owning your career growth is setting clear, actionable goals. Just like setting goals for learning new skills or completing projects, career goals should be well-defined and measurable. The **SMART framework** (Specific, Measurable, Achievable, Relevant, and Time-bound) is a proven method for setting goals that are attainable and meaningful.

For example, instead of setting a vague goal like "I want to be promoted," break it down: "I will develop leadership skills by completing a management course and leading a small team project within the next six months." This specific goal has measurable milestones and a deadline, which makes it easier to track progress.

Measuring and Tracking Your Progress

There Is No Such Thing as Job Security; There Is Skill Security

To ensure continuous improvement, it's essential to regularly **measure** and **track** your career growth. This involves evaluating both your hard skills (technical abilities) and soft skills (communication, leadership, teamwork, etc.). In fact, research by **LinkedIn Learning** found that soft skills such as adaptability, emotional intelligence, and time management are increasingly valued in the workplace, with 92% of talent professionals considering soft skills just as important as hard skills.

1. Self-Assessment and Peer Feedback

One of the most effective ways to measure career growth is through regular **self-assessment**. Ask yourself key questions: What skills have I developed over the past year? What areas need improvement? What feedback have I received from colleagues or supervisors?

Requesting feedback from peers, mentors, or supervisors is invaluable in identifying strengths and areas for improvement. According to **Harvard Business Review**, feedback is one of the most powerful tools for professional development. Employees who actively seek feedback are more likely to see measurable improvements in their performance and are often perceived as more committed to their roles.

2. Tracking Hard Skills and Certifications

There Is No Such Thing as Job Security; There Is Skill Security

Hard skills can be easily measured by the completion of certifications, training programs, and the application of technical skills in the workplace. Keeping a **skills portfolio** or **track record** of your achievements, projects, and certifications will allow you to clearly see your growth over time. Many industries, such as IT, marketing, and project management, require continuous education and certifications (e.g., **Google Analytics, AWS Solutions Architect, PMP Certification**) to stay competitive.

A **PwC report** found that professionals who continuously update their hard skills and earn certifications are not only more likely to remain employed but also tend to have higher earning potential, with certified professionals earning up to **20% more** than their uncertified counterparts.

3. Tracking Soft Skills Development

Measuring soft skills can be more challenging, but it's equally important. Start by identifying which soft skills are most critical for your role or desired career path—communication, leadership, negotiation, problem-solving, etc. You can track improvements in soft skills through peer reviews, self-reflection, or even asking colleagues for feedback on specific aspects like collaboration or emotional intelligence.

There Is No Such Thing as Job Security; There Is Skill Security

For example, if you want to improve public speaking skills, you can track your progress by participating in **Toastmasters International** or other speaking engagements, receiving feedback, and noting improvements over time.

Monitoring Your Impact in the Workplace

Another way to measure career growth is to assess your impact on your organization. Evaluate how your work contributes to the company's goals or mission. Are you delivering projects on time? Are you leading successful initiatives or driving revenue? **Quantifying your achievements** (e.g., improving a process that saves time, increasing sales by a certain percentage) will not only help you track your growth but also provide tangible evidence during performance reviews.

The Role of Continuous Improvement in Career Growth

The key to sustained career growth lies in the mindset of **continuous improvement**. Whether you're at the beginning of your career or already a seasoned professional, there's always room for growth. A **study by Deloitte** showed that employees who engage in continuous learning are more likely to feel satisfied in their roles and are better equipped to handle workplace challenges.

There Is No Such Thing as Job Security; There Is Skill Security

Developing a **growth mindset**, as coined by Carol Dweck, means believing that your abilities can be developed through effort and learning. People with a growth mindset embrace challenges, persist in the face of setbacks, and see failures as opportunities for growth. This attitude is crucial in taking ownership of your career.

1. Learning from Setbacks and Failures

Every career is bound to have its ups and downs, and setbacks are inevitable. However, how you respond to challenges defines your growth. **Failure** is often one of the greatest teachers, providing valuable lessons in resilience, problem-solving, and self-awareness. When you take ownership of your career, you accept failures as part of the learning process.

In fact, many of the world's most successful leaders have experienced significant career setbacks before achieving greatness. **Walt Disney**, for instance, was fired from a newspaper job for "lacking imagination" before he went on to create one of the most successful media empires in history. By reframing setbacks as learning experiences, you can cultivate resilience and perseverance.

2. Creating a Personal Development Plan

A **Personal Development Plan (PDP)** is a structured and intentional approach to self-improvement. It outlines the skills, knowledge, and experiences you aim to acquire,

There Is No Such Thing as Job Security; There Is Skill Security

along with specific actions to achieve these goals. Your PDP should be dynamic, meaning it evolves as your career grows.

A good PDP includes short-term, medium-term, and long-term goals, as well as the steps needed to reach them. For example, a short-term goal might be to complete a leadership training course, a medium-term goal could be to take on a management role within your department, and a long-term goal might be to become a senior executive. Regularly reviewing and updating your PDP helps you stay on track and measure your progress.

Maximizing Self-Worth and Career Identity

Taking ownership of your career also involves cultivating a strong sense of **self-worth** and career identity. Your career is not just about the roles you hold or the salary you earn—it's about the value you bring to your work and the sense of purpose you derive from it.

1. Building Self-Esteem Through Skill Mastery

Mastering new skills boosts self-esteem by reinforcing a sense of competence and achievement. Whether it's mastering a new programming language or becoming a more effective communicator, each step in skill acquisition strengthens your self-confidence. As **Forbes** reported, employees who continuously develop their skills and seek

There Is No Such Thing as Job Security; There Is Skill Security

growth opportunities are more likely to feel confident in their roles and take on leadership positions.

2. Aligning Career Growth with Personal Values

True career satisfaction comes from aligning your professional growth with your personal values and long-term goals. Are you passionate about leadership? Innovation? Making an impact in your community? Understanding what motivates you on a deeper level allows you to pursue roles and projects that resonate with your core values.

Studies by **Harvard Business School** show that individual who align their work with their values report higher job satisfaction and are less likely to experience burnout. When you own your career growth, you ensure that your professional path aligns with your personal identity and long-term vision.

Practical Steps to Own Your Career Growth

1. **Regularly Review and Reflect on Progress**: Set aside time every quarter to reflect on your career growth. Have you achieved the goals you set? What challenges have you faced? What new opportunities have emerged? Reflection helps you stay grounded and ensures that you're continuously moving in the right direction.

There Is No Such Thing as Job Security; There Is Skill Security

2. **Document Your Achievements**: Keep a running list of your accomplishments, both big and small. This might include successful projects, new skills, awards, or leadership roles. Documenting achievements not only helps during performance reviews but also reinforces your sense of progress.

3. **Seek Opportunities for Growth**: Be proactive in seeking out new opportunities for learning and growth, whether it's through formal training, mentorship, or taking on stretch assignments at work. The more you expose yourself to new challenges, the more you'll grow.

4. **Network and Build Relationships**: Building a strong professional network is essential for career growth. Surround yourself with mentors, peers, and industry experts who can provide guidance, feedback, and support. A **Harvard Business Review** study found that professionals with strong networks are more likely to be promoted and achieve career success.

Conclusion: Taking Ownership of Your Career

In conclusion, owning your career growth means actively setting clear goals, tracking progress, and continuously improving your skills. By measuring your development in both hard and soft skills, seeking feedback, and aligning

There Is No Such Thing as Job Security; There Is Skill Security

your professional journey with your values, you can ensure sustained progress and fulfillment in your career. Taking ownership not only boosts self-esteem and self-worth but also positions you for long-term success, regardless of industry changes. Your career is in your hands, and with the right mindset, continuous improvement becomes a pathway to thriving professionally.

**There Is No Such Thing as Job Security;
There Is Skill Security**

Embracing Self: The True Identity Beyond Jobs – A Dedication to Brian Keinsley and Thomas Noland

As I conclude this chapter, I want to express my heartfelt gratitude to my mentors, Brian Keinsley and Thomas Noland, whose guidance shaped me into the professional and person I am today. This book is written with immense respect for their impact on my life. Brian, especially, you have been an unwavering source of belief and support, a reflection of what makes the USA the incredible nation it is—a place of opportunity and mentorship.

This book was born from the emotions I feel mourning their loss, but it is also a reflection on the broader truths of life and work. Too often, we attach our identity to our job titles, our bosses, or the corporations we work for, forgetting that our true value lies within us—our skills, emotions, habits, and the networks we build. Our identity is not our job, it is the **truth** of who we are.

In today's world of AI, where data can reveal all that is false or wasteful, the most important asset we own is our truth—our authenticity, our self-worth, and the value we add to others. As my 7-year-old son, Dylan, once said when I asked, "Who do you love most?" expecting him to say

There Is No Such Thing as Job Security; There Is Skill Security

"Dad," he replied, "I love myself the most." Amusing and wise beyond his years, Dylan's words remind us that self-love is the foundation for loving others. When we nurture ourselves, we can contribute so much more to the world around us.

As I dedicate this book to my mentors and to all who have shaped me, I emphasize the importance of spiritual connection and self-visualization. It is through knowing ourselves, valuing ourselves, and taking action from a place of love and truth that we can add the most value to others. This journey is not selfish; it's about becoming the best version of ourselves to serve others better. To Brian and Thomas, you believed in me, and I carry that belief forward into every chapter of my life. Thank you.

**There Is No Such Thing as Job Security;
There Is Skill Security**

POEM: God, Life is Short

God, life is short as You give to each of us,
A fleeting chance to experience, to grow, to trust.
Yet we filter down, limiting our view,
Seeing only our job, forgetting what's true.

The world, the work beyond our task,
Is the deeper truth we fail to ask.
Thank You for the strength You give within,
Guide us to expand, not shrink, our vision thin.

Let us rise to our God-given might,
Not bound by human limits, but divine light.
To add value each day to self and life,
Through love, purpose, and overcoming strife.

We exhaust our bodies, but let us see,
Our spirit thrives, empowered, and free.
When we leave this earth, let us tell,
Of the value we've added, the stories we dwell.

True purpose found, not filtered small,
But held in Your grace, standing tall.
Let our work and actions be the gift we give,
So we may speak of life lived, when with You, we live.

**There Is No Such Thing as Job Security;
There Is Skill Security**

The End

Thank You

"There is nothing that belongs to you that you don't create yourself." - Di Tran

www.ingramcontent.com/pod-product-compliance
Lightning Source LLC
Chambersburg PA
CBHW052208220526
45471CB00004B/1871